This is my faith journey.

_____

The Gift of Invitation: 7 Ways That Jesus Invites You to a Life of Grace

Nihil obstat:
   Rev. Timothy Hall,
   Censor librorum
   September 15, 2018

Imprimatur:
   †Most Rev. John M. Quinn,
   Bishop of Winona
   September 15, 2018

24 23 22 21 20 19   2 3 4 5 6 7 8 9

Cover, interior design and composition by Laurie Nelson, Agápe Design Studios.
Graphic elements: © iStockphoto.com, © Adobe Stock

Copy editing by Karen Carter.

ISBN: 978-1-68192-499-1 (Inventory No. T2388)
LCCN: 2019939975

Stay Connected Journals for Catholic Women are published by Our Sunday Visitor Publishing Division, 200 Noll Plaza, Huntington, IN 46750; 1-800-348-2440; www.osv.com.

Acknowledgments

Scripture texts in this work are taken from the New American Bible, revised edition © 2010, 1991, 1986, 1970 Confraternity of Christian Doctrine, Washington, D.C. and are used by permission of the copyright owner. All Rights Reserved. No part of the New American Bible may be reproduced in any form without permission in writing from the copyright owner.

Quotes from the Catechism of the Catholic Church are taken from the English translation of the Catechism of the Catholic Church for the United States of America, 2nd ed. Copyright 1997 by United States Catholic Conference—Libreria Editrice Vaticana.

Journals for Catholic Women

The Gift of Invitation:

7 Ways Jesus Invites You to a Life of Grace

Allison Gingras

Much love and many thanks to:

my wicked awesome family for supporting my heart's desires:
Kevin, Ian, Adam, and Faith

my incredible spiritual director: Deacon Gerald Ryan

the village that helped sort through my comma challenges:
Maria, Tiffany, Deanna, Laure, Elizabeth, Shannon, and Patsy

my #SaintPosse for always having my back: Ven. Patrick
Peyton, Bl. Solanus Casey, Bl. Stanley Rother, St. Thérèse,
St. Faustina, my (hardworking) guardian angel, and Mary,
Our Lady of Grace

A very special thanks to Gracewatch Media for taking on my
crazy idea.

Table of Contents

Introduction

The best place to begin explaining *The Gift of Invitation* and the *Stay Connected Journals for Catholic Women* is to share the parable of the sower. Why? Discovering the important role of the Word of God in my faith journey was the inspiration behind the creation of a book series that provides women with a simple, engaging, and Scripture-rich opportunity to stay connected to Jesus and to their faith through the beauty of self-reflection and fellowship with others. After a decade of participating in women's faith-sharing groups, I have come to recognize elements of this parable in everyone's spiritual journey.

Parable of the Farmer Scattering Seed

When a large crowd gathered, with people from one town after another journeying to him, he spoke in a parable. "A sower went out to sow his seed. And as he sowed, some seed fell on the path and was trampled, and the birds of the sky ate it up. Some seed fell on rocky ground, and when it grew, it withered for lack of moisture. Some seed fell among thorns, and the thorns grew with it and choked it. And some seed fell on good soil, and when it grew, it produced fruit a hundredfold." After saying this, he called out, "Whoever has ears to hear ought to hear."

The Purpose of the Parables

Then his disciples asked him what the meaning of this parable might be. He answered, "Knowledge of the mysteries of the kingdom of God has been granted to you; but to the rest, they are made known through parables so that 'they may look but not see, and hear but not understand.'"

The Parable of the Sower Explained

This is the meaning of the parable. The seed is the word of God. Those on the path are the ones who have heard, but the devil comes and takes away the word from their hearts that they may not believe and be saved. Those on rocky ground are the ones who, when they hear, receive the word with joy, but they have no root; they believe only for a time and fall away in time of trial. As for the seed that fell among thorns, they are the ones who have heard, but as they go along, they are choked by the anxieties and riches and pleasures of life, and they fail to produce mature fruit. But as for the seed that fell on rich soil, they are the ones who, when they have heard the word, embrace it with a generous and good heart, and bear fruit through perseverance. (Luke 8:4–15)

Sometimes I wish I were as astute in the present as I am in hindsight. I suppose I am not alone in that desire. I only discovered the transformative power of the Word of God in my spiritual development after reflecting on this parable. Spending time with the Scriptures helped me overcome so many obstacles I had in living the Catholic faith. The distance from Jesus I once complained about, the lack of understanding why I would want to follow God's "rules," and even being motivated to make more time for faith in my life, were all issues that I found answers for in the Scriptures. As equally important for me was having others to share my faith experience with. Many of my spiritual aha moments came during small group sharing; however, it would take a few sowings before these seeds would take.

When I was a child, my parents brought my siblings and me to Sunday Mass. The Catholic Mass is steeped in Scriptures, yet somehow I completely missed this important fact. I have to sheepishly admit that it was not until my mid-thirties that I realized the readings, the responsorial psalm, the prayers, and even the music all came directly from or were inspired by the Scriptures. I'm not exactly sure where the communication breakdown took place, but the fact remains that the seeds, the Word of God, had been scattered before me. However, like the seeds strewn on the rocky path in the parable, although the Word had reached my ears, the devil took full advantage of my ignorance and snatched the meaning away before it could penetrate my heart.

As an adult, responsible for fostering my own faith life, I attempted to grow spiritually by attending many retreat programs. On retreat, my heart would be set on fire for the things of God, especially while participating in Mass. All my senses seemed to be heightened—the incense smelled sweeter, the readings felt more inspired, the homilies touched deep into my heart as if they were written just for me, even kneeling in prayer felt more reverent. I left ready to live a life centered on Jesus, to give him everything; each time I truly intended to stay connected.

3

Filled with this renewed desire to become closer to God, I vowed to pray the Rosary daily, attend Mass more faithfully, and not give into my fears by continuing to avoid the sacrament of Reconciliation. For a little while following these retreat experiences, I sang a little louder in church, made time for prayer at home, and even subscribed to a Catholic magazine. Yep, I was ready to be all in!

Yet, over time all those things I had discovered to nourish my budding faith—the encouraging retreat team, consistent study of the Scriptures, and quiet time for prayer—faded. I did not stick with anything long enough to develop deep roots of faith, and my attention to God withered away. I was left with a thirst for something, and because I was unable to duplicate the euphoric feelings of my retreat experiences, I abandoned the work of cultivating a meaningful relationship with Jesus.

Trying to fill the emptiness, I busied myself being a wife, mother (nurse, counselor, teacher, cook, housekeeper, chauffeur), and even dabbled in a variety of careers. These were all good things, important roles and responsibilities that I am sure pleased the Lord, but without including him in them, I was missing the fullness of joy available to me.

The thorns of this world grew all around me. Any seeds dropped by priests, friends, or the occasional inspirational speaker would be washed away by the flood of daily worries, concerns, and tasks. Time spent with any religious reading materials—books, magazines, the

Bible—would cease to exist. I had hardly enough time to read bedtime stories to my children, never mind the Bible, which I struggled to understand anyway. Prayer would consist of a quick blessing before meals, a quick petition as I tried to make our income cover our expenses, or an Our Father or Hail Mary as I was drifting off to sleep, which I probably prayed more out of habit than faith.

The one thing that did remain consistent was my weekly attendance at Mass, but not because I experienced spiritual growth from it. I was convinced that perfect attendance at Mass was a good heavenly insurance policy. I imagined that St. Peter checked off my name in some celestial attendance book, so if my plan to volunteer my way into heaven failed to work, at least I had that perfect attendance record to present. Well, that is how I had it all figured out anyway in the little

time I had to think about these things between my kids' activities, board meetings, school commitments, and social engagements. The thorns of my cluttered calendar would choke out the tender saplings of my faith trying to reach the sun (or Son, as the case may be), leaving me with very little opportunity for the Word of God to dwell in me richly (Colossians 3:16).

A simple invitation from a friend to join a small faith-sharing group in her home cultivated the rich soil in my heart, preparing me to embrace the Word of God and be transformed. That invitation was so life-changing it inspired me to want to share it with others, in hopes that they, too, would accept and extend invitations to develop their relationships with Jesus through study of the Word. As I grew closer to Christ, I realized that the invitation my friend had extended to me was actually Jesus' invitation extended through her. My time in this small faith-sharing group helped me recognize and accept Jesus' invitations to come and see, to know him better, and to follow his model of faith. These sweet summonses are offered in the Scriptures, in our hearts through our Baptism, and through the care and love of others (see *Catechism* 2013). Incredible blessings abound when you share your faith journey with others; sometimes it is just a matter of knowing which row to till.

Even rich soil needs consistent tending in order for seedlings to continue to flourish within it. Weeds of distraction, busyness, and apathy must be constantly pulled, or they will completely overtake our time with the Lord. Fertilizing the soil is critical. Our faith is watered and nurtured by, what I call, the "grace trifecta," which consists of daily participation in prayer, sacrament, and Scripture, along with the blessings that come from spiritual reading especially in the context of a faith-sharing group.

I pray that the soil of your heart will be well nourished by *The Gift of Invitation* and the entire *Stay Connected* faith-sharing series. I pray it is nurtured not only by your reading and your private time with Jesus, but also by the fellow gardeners in your faith-sharing group. May your faith grow deep sustaining roots. May your time together in the Word of God ward off everything that seeks to devour the seeds of faith Jesus is planting in your life. May the sharing of your faith journey help you to stay connected and be lead ever closer to Jesus and to heaven. And may you flourish in the warmth of the Son.

1: Invitation to Come and See

INVITATION

Opening Prayer

Jesus, I pray that I will accept your remarkable invitation to come and see, yet I begin with a little fear and trepidation. Thank you for inspiring me to continually seek how to best follow you. While I believe my Baptism provided me a place in your heavenly family, it is not always easy to see myself as a beloved daughter of God. As I begin this study of your many gracious invitations, I ask for every blessing and grace to understand how each relates personally to me. I pray for the wisdom and understanding to allow your Word to draw me closer to you.

Lord Jesus, since you have brought me to this book, I believe you have something special for me within its pages. Open my heart and mind to receive the messages that you have reserved here especially for me.

You delight in granting me the desires of my heart. Allow me to see clearly what you desire for me to learn, whether in your word, in sharing with others, or in the silence of my prayers. May this study help me begin to see what that desire is so that I may witness your love and generosity in my life. May this time with you prepare me not only to accept your invitation but also to

9

extend one to allow you into my everyday, ordinary moments of life. Most importantly, may I grow to understand how your invitations are opportunities to embrace the abundant life you came to give me. Amen.

On My Heart:

_____

_____

_____

_____

_____

_____

_____

_____

_____

_____

Invitation to Come and See

Although my parents sought to promptly baptize me just one week after my birth on July 14th, 1968, we weren't really a family that regularly practiced their faith. The memories of my family praying together or attending Mass are few. In fact, although I am sure we did, I have no recollection of us attending services together as a family of five. One of my most vivid Christmas memories comes from sitting at the bottom of our basement stairs waiting for my dad to come home from Christmas Eve Mass. Our family tradition was to open one gift on Christmas Eve, and I could hardly wait. That year, my mother had purchased the number one item on my wish list, a Barbie beautician doll—a nearly life-sized head with a full set of hair to style along with blue eyeshadow and pink rouge to apply to her face. It came in a telltale hexagon box, which my mother did very little to mask in her wrapping. This seemingly endless waiting marks the start of my long-held notion that Mass dragged on forever.

My most unforgettable childhood church memory involves my brother, a rhyming name of a dearly departed woman, and one of the worst punishments of my life. During the Prayer of the Faithful, an intention was offered for one, "Merry Perry." It was one of those moments when you know it is best not to make eye contact with your sibling. You know that moment between an uncontrollable giggle fit and maintaining your composure is in delicate balance. Yet, you cannot help yourself. You shoot your brother that knowing glance, and then fight for the next ten minutes to squelch the giggles. You bite your tongue, try praying, pinch the back of your arm, all to no avail. The laughter bursts forth, the tears stream down your face, and the next thing you know, watching television is gone for a month!

No Experience Necessary

My experiences of praying at home as a child were limited. As a small child I remember kneeling on a little convertible stool with the Now I Lay Me Down to Sleep prayer stenciled on it. You know the one in which we tell kids there is a possibility they will die in their sleep, and then wonder why they won't go to sleep. We only prayed as a family during thunderstorms. My father worked evenings, and my mother was petrified of storms. She would unplug everything in the house (Remember when you could do that?) and then line the three children on the couch to pray the Rosary. Then my house was struck by lightning, true story. We never prayed again after that.

Jesus to me was the baby in the manger and the man on the cross. There was no talk of Jesus as brother, friend, teacher, shepherd, or even savior. We were not Bible-reading Catholic Christians, so his words were unknown to me. Infrequent church attendance, poor attention in catechism classes, and a lack of home education of the faith left me ignorant of who Jesus really is and, more importantly, who he wanted to be in my life.

Saint Augustine said, "You have made us for Yourself, and our hearts are restless until they find their rest in You."[1] We are created with a God-sized hole in our hearts. Unaware that this longing had a name, I tried for most of my life to fill it with shiny things, tasty food, or constant chatter. Most of my life was spent buying what I could not afford, eating more than my fill, and sharing more information than I should. After years of this behavior, I still found myself feeling empty and searching for something to fill the void. The invitation to come and see did not come directly from Jesus, like it did to the disciples in the Bible, but from one of his faithful followers.

The Honor of Your Presence

In December 2004, I was running a preschool in my home. The mother of one of my students had also become a friend from church. For Christmas, she gave me *The Purpose Driven Life* by Rick Warren. Along with the gift came an invitation to attend Bible study at her home. I laughed softly and innocently said, "But we are Catholic; we don't read the Bible." Enthralled by her enthusiasm and feeling a bit obliged because of her kind gift, I agreed to go. In my head, I was going for one week. What's that old saying, "We plan and God laughs"?

Week one came. I went. She had really yummy snacks. I came back the second week for more guac and cookies. Each week, the book brought us deeper and deeper into communion with Christ through his Word. Jesus ceased to be a two-dimensional figure connected to a couple of holidays. Jesus became brother, friend, teacher, shepherd, and, most of all, Savior.

The Beauty of Adoption

Through our Baptism, "we are freed from sin and reborn as sons of God; we become members of Christ, are incorporated into the Church and made sharers in her mission" (*Catechism*, 1213). In fact, the opening prayer at Mass for Sunday the Twenty-Third Week of Ordinary Time reminds us of this: "O God, by whom we are redeemed and receive adoption, look graciously upon your beloved sons and daughters...." This concept of being adopted by God really hit home when I became an adoptive mom in 2009. At the time of my daughter Faith's adoption, we already had two biological sons. I worried if I would be capable of loving my new daughter in the same unconditional way that I loved my boys. I had known them from the moment of their conception. How could I possibly love this little girl I was going to meet at nearly four years old?

I brought this concern to prayer often and would receive reassurance again and again. I had an overwhelming sense of peace, an internal message from God saying, "Don't worry; you can do this." Once united with my daughter, I never once felt anything but a complete bond with her. Although Faith's transition into our family came with a few bumps, her assimilation into our hearts did not.

Years later, as I was contemplating this idea of being an adopted daughter of God, the fullness and beauty of what that meant in light of my own experiences overwhelmed me. It was in realizing how if I, a faulted and weak human being, could love my daughter so fully, how much more then could the God of the Universe love us. Furthermore, it did not take us long to drop the word "adopted" from how we iden-tified our daughter. When I introduce her, I simply say, "This is my daughter, Faith." Through our Baptism, we unequivocally become the beloved and cherished children of God the Father Almighty. And just as I grew ever closer to Faith, so too are we called "toward ever more intimate union with Christ" (*Catechism*, 2014).

An Invitation to Ponder

Jesus calls all of us into relationship with him. Have you experienced him asking you to "come and see," or to "follow me"? If so, can you describe the invitation? How have you responded to it? Are you able to see yourself as a true daughter of God the Father?

_____

_____

_____

_____

_____

_____

_____

_____

_____

_____

_____

_____

_____

Connecting to Scripture

In my (somewhat humble) opinion, this is the best section of the whole journal. It is my favorite part because I absolutely cherish spending time contemplating the Word of God. At the heart of my reversion journey in 2005 was the unexpected joy of being introduced to the daily reading of the Scriptures. Being privy to the teachings of Christ and getting a glimpse of the thoughts of God through these divinely inspired words deepened my faith in ways I never could have imagined.

I can honestly say I have never emerged from my time with the Scriptures without some message, inspiration, or call to action. If you have ever longed to hear Jesus speak to you but feel that he remains silent, the Word of God is truly the best place to start. I recommend purchasing a Bible with a good Catholic commentary[2] to help guide your time with Scripture; you will find it a wonderful complement to your personal reflections.

Take time to read each Scripture passage referenced below (and in each of the subsequent chapters), and pay special attention to what the Holy Spirit is calling your attention to in each verse. Do not concern yourself with right or wrong responses; simply relax and allow yourself to truly enjoy this time with the Word of God. Be assured, Jesus has no expectations for your time together; there is no perfect rubric for your time with Jesus, whether you are in prayer, reading Scriptures, or participating in the sacraments. The beauty of the *Stay Connected* faith-sharing series[3] is that the time you spend with these books is your prayer time. Each of these journals is designed to be a guide for a personal encounter with the Triune God—Father, Son, and Holy Spirit.

If you wish, read each verse a few times, asking the Holy Spirit to guide your heart and mind to receive what he has prepared just for you. Use the space provided under each Scripture verse to note any inspirations or thoughts that come to you as you read. Share your thoughts with a small group or maintain your notes as a personal reflection.

PRAYER TO THE HOLY SPIRIT BEFORE READING SCRIPTURE:

Come Holy Spirit. Fill me with every grace and blessing necessary to understand the message, prepared and awaiting me, in the Scriptures. May I grow deeper in faith, in hope, and in love with Jesus as I spend this time with the Word of God. Amen.

⌇ Isaiah 45:3 and 45:5-6 _____

_____

_____

⌇ Matthew 3:13-17 _____

_____

_____

⌇ Luke 6:37-38 _____

_____

_____

↗ John 1:36–51 _____

_____

_____

↗ John 20:29 _____

_____

_____

Scripture Reflection

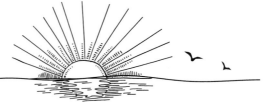

"What are you looking for?" (John 1:38) Jesus asks, and then he offers a simple invitation to come and see. Jesus' invitation begins with a prompt for us to consider what we are looking for. Without receiving a response and knowing he has everything we seek, he invites us to come and see. Some of the disciples we encounter in Scripture stayed because they had heard Jesus preach. Peter came to see after his brother, Andrew, had heard and invited him to see for himself. It was Andrew's evangelization that brought Peter to seek the Lord. We will experience this on our own road to discipleship. Some will come to Christ in response to invitations from others who are already following him. Some may come to follow Jesus through a personal encounter. And still others will come in response to an invitation or witness of another person, but will decide to stay because that invitation leads to a personal encounter with Christ.

Jesus' invitation is no different for us today than it was for the disciples. He still seeks to have us come and see. There will be obstacles, much like those the disciples themselves faced. There will be commitments to work and family and the feeling of being too busy with pressing tasks and obligations to come and see. Jesus did not make arguments or try to force what he knew was best for them. Instead, he merely extended his invitation again for them to come and see.

My Prayer for You

That is what I pray the *Stay Connected* series[4] does for you. Each chapter is a gentle summons to make time each week to come and see. It is an opportunity to put aside the obstacles that continue to keep you from following Christ as fully as God intended when he created you, to open up the Scriptures, and to let Jesus speak to your heart.

One of the questions I'm often asked is how do I hear Jesus speaking to me? I honestly never did until I spent time in his Word, in prayer, and in full participation in the sacraments—"grace trifecta." Only after making it a priority to live a life built on this firm foundation did I begin hearing Jesus speak to my heart. In those beautiful traditions and practices of faith, Jesus showed me how to follow him. I needed to leave behind my love of gossip, my penchant for judging others, and my tendency toward extreme busyness (some of those I am still working on) to follow Jesus more closely. It has been over ten years. I have not regretted a single moment, nor have I missed those things to which I had clung so tightly and which had kept me from coming to see.

A Doubting Thomas Like Me

After his resurrection, the apostle Thomas struggled to believe that Jesus was alive. He needed physical evidence in order to accept that Jesus had actually resurrected from the dead (John 20:24–31). Jesus was not angry with his request; he appeared, allowed Thomas the opportunity to put his fingers into Jesus' hands and his hand into Jesus' side, and said gently, "Do not be unbelieving, but believe" (John 20:27). What Jesus said next is one of my favorite lines in all of Scripture: "Have you come to believe because you have seen me? Blessed are those who have not seen and have believed" (John 20:29).

I am so much like Thomas in that I need to see and feel and touch in order to believe. I seek signs and wonders within my day-to-day life to prove to myself that Jesus is real and with me. I am grateful that Jesus seems to have pity on me, and is, also, quite generous in responding. He brings into my everyday life an abundance of what I call "godcidences"—what the world would see as coincidence, yet when you look at the situation through the eyes of faith, you cannot miss the hand of God at work within it (more on that in later chapters), and it is hard to imagine my requests make him angry. Like the centurion in Mark's Gospel, I have often said to Jesus, "I do believe, help my unbelief!" (Mark 9:24)

As we journey together through this book, I will share some of the amazing ways the Lord has made himself present in my life. I hope that my story helps you to see Jesus present in your own life. It is my hope and my prayer that by the conclusion of *The Gift of Invitation* you, too, begin to recognize the gift of grace that God confers into our everyday, ordinary lives.

An Invitation to Share

1. Baptism is a big step toward accepting the invitation from Jesus to "come and see" and to "follow me." For some it came of their own choosing and for others it was a choice made by their parents.

Either way, it is often considered the second most important day in our lives, some might even say it is the most important. Pope Francis, during his April 11, 2018, Wednesday Audience, encouraged everyone to not only know the date of their baptism but celebrate it:

Therefore, Baptism is a rebirth. I am certain, quite sure, that we all remember our date of birth: certain. But I ask myself, a little doubtfully, and I ask you: do each of you recall the date of your Baptism? Some say "yes"—okay. But it is a rather weak "yes", because perhaps many do not remember this date. But if we celebrate birthdays, why not celebrate—or at least remember—the day of rebirth? I will give you a homework assignment, a task to do today at home. Those of you who do not remember the date of your Baptism, ask your mother, aunts and uncles, nieces and nephews, ask them: "Do you know the date of my Baptism?"; and never forget it. And thank the Lord for that day, because it is the very day on which Jesus entered me, the Holy Spirit entered me. Do you understand what your homework is? We should all know the date of our Baptism. It is another birthday: the date of rebirth. Do not forget to do this, please.

Do you remember the date of your Baptism? Have you ever considered celebrating this important day in your life? If you already do, share how. What does Baptism mean to you?

_____

_____

_____

_____

_____

_____

_____

_____

2. Some of Jesus' disciples followed him because they encountered him themselves. Others followed after learning about him from a friend. Still others heard of him but did not choose to follow until they had encountered Jesus for themselves. Which of these three experiences do you feel most closely relates to the beginning of your relationship with Christ?

_____

_____

_____

_____

_____

_____

_____

_____

_____

_____

_____

3. When I first started to feel the call from Christ to come and know him better, I resisted. I was so afraid of what he was going to ask me to give up. The first obstacle I had to overcome was my attachment to gossip. It wasn't easy to let go, but once I did, I found better topics for conversation. While there are still temptations to resist and habits I need to work on, I feel that overcoming that first obstacle opened my heart to saying yes to following Jesus. What attachments do you think are keeping you from knowing Christ better?

_____

_____

_____

_____

_____

_____

_____

_____

_____

_____

_____

Closing Prayer

At my Baptism, I began a beautiful journey of faith with you, O Lord. In Baptism, I began to respond to your invitation to join a new *heavenly family. I have been graciously adopted with full rights to the inheritance of eternal life through grace. I have been given the great opportunity to know, love, and serve you, in this world and especially in the next.*

You've invited me to prayer so that I may be in constant communication with you. This daily chat will teach me how to better discern your plans for me. Lord, help me to call upon the grace of my Baptism every day so I may be reminded of the glorious promises that come with it. Let me neither grow weary of prayer nor fear that I have been abandoned.

In my Baptism, I was sealed as your child. I have been cleansed of my original sin, which separated me from you. Redeemed by the cross, I boldly proclaim your love for me as I work out my salvation. This invitation from you overwhelms me at times. I am so thankful that you have made me yours. As I continue in this study, I feel a little like a baby bird with my loving mama nudging me towards the edge of the nest. I long to soar with you, but I'm unsure of how to do that. I have a great fear of plummeting in failure. Your promises reassure me, and I embrace them, Lord, with all my heart. I pray for the grace to believe this nudge towards a closer relationship and deeper faith comes with a new found trust and hope. Unless I spread my wings and take a chance, I will never discover the abundant life you set before me.

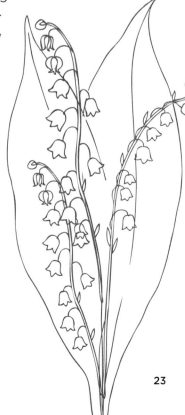

Dear Lord, be with me in my reading and reflection as I grow ever closer to you. Amen.

2: Invitation to Take His Yoke

INVITATION

Opening Prayer

Jesus, you have presented me with an invitation to take your yoke upon me. Honestly, Lord, I am unsure of what you are truly asking but overjoyed that this invitation comes with a promise of rest for my weary soul. You are acutely aware of all my fears, anxieties, and worries. While my life is filled with an abundance of blessings, it also contains a surplus of difficulties.

I am grateful that you offer to bear my burdens, however, my intuition tells me there is a much greater blessing with this invitation. A rabbi's yoke was his teachings. As I read your words in the Gospels, you teach me to listen to your Father, show me how to respond to others, and model a life of faith for me. Help me to boldly accept this invitation to learn from you.

Your invitation to "come and see" remains on my heart as I move ever deeper into relationship with you into a relationship with you. Please, dispel my trepidations and insecurities; remind me again and again that you would never ask the impossible. Lord, show me how to take your yoke upon myself. Show me how to learn from you, and most of all, dear Jesus, please give rest to my weary soul. Amen.

On My Heart

Invitation to Take His Yoke

At least once a year, I try to go on retreat. It is good to get away from the noise of everyday life to contemplate the things of heaven. It is remarkable what Jesus can teach you when you have time to be attentive. One retreat, during morning prayer, we were invited by the prayer leader to close our eyes. We were then instructed to imagine ourselves standing with Jesus next to a horse. We were going to take a gentle horseback ride together. First, each of us and Jesus needed to mount the horse. At that point, the prayer leader paused and asked us to note where we saw ourselves sitting in relation to Jesus. Were we behind or in front of Jesus? Who had the reins? *Gulp!* With my eyes closed, still deep in this visualization exercise, I saw very clearly—I had the reins.

We took turns sharing the results of our visualization exercise. While I was not the only woman who had placed herself in front of Jesus on the horse, I was the only one who had grabbed the reins. The outcome of this exercise was very telling. I want Jesus along for the ride, but I have a really hard time letting go of control. My prayer is often, "My will be done." I lack trust in God's plans for my life. I struggle to see the truth: God's will for me is always for my good, and allowing myself to rest in that knowledge will always lead me to peace. I wonder how many times a day Jesus shakes his head in dismay at how difficult I make things on myself by not allowing him to take the reins. How can I believe he is the Son of God, which I do, yet be incapable of trusting him completely with my life?

A year later, I found myself back on retreat sitting quietly in Eucharistic adoration with only my Bible. I prayed, reading a passage here and there, just waiting for the Holy Spirit to inspire me. My eyes fell upon Matthew 11:28–30, and I read, "Come to Me, all who are weary and heavy-laden, and I will give you rest. Take My yoke upon you and learn from Me, for I am gentle and humble in heart, and YOU WILL FIND REST FOR YOUR SOULS. For My yoke is easy and My burden is light."[5] The section capitalized in the Bible version of the App I was using caused me to pause. Did Jesus have to resort to yelling to get my attention? The words "rest for my soul" cut to the marrow of my bones. How lovely freedom from my burdens would be! Cue Jesus' face-palm as I continue to miss the point. Then I remembered the imaginary horse ride and my hands gripped tightly around the reins. Jesus whispered into my heart, "You can have peace and rest, even joy, Allison; just let go of the reins!"

The Multifaceted Yoke

For the remainder of the retreat, I pondered what exactly Jesus meant by this easy yoke he had for me. What was it precisely? How could I possibly take it upon myself if I had no idea what it was I would be taking? So just as I do for everything else I do not understand, I Googled it. How did I ever survive before Google? *The Oxford American College Dictionary* informed me that a yoke is "a wooden cross-piece that is fastened over the necks of two animals and attached to the plow or cart that they are to pull."

The oxen are yoked together to lighten their work burden. Jesus and I could be tandem work horses plowing through the world's trials and troubles. That would surely lighten my burden. Yet, I sensed there was more to be learned. So back to Google I went. This second research attempt yielded a picture of a single wooden yolk with reins. I'm not going to lie; when I saw the reins attached to the yolk in the picture, I laughed out loud. As I gazed upon the image of the single yolk, I felt Jesus softly whisper into my heart, "Put my yoke upon you, let me direct your steps, so you can learn from me. Trust me to lead you to pastures of rest and peace. I am trustworthy. My yoke is, indeed, easy because it is one constructed out of pure love of you."

Just a few days later, I was speaking with a dear friend, who also happens to be a Scripture scholar. I shared my experience with Matthew's Gospel in adoration, my yoke research, and my resulting aha moments. She then informed me of another, ancient meaning, of *yoke*. In the time of Jesus' earthly life, when a person took on the teaching of the rabbi, it was said that they took upon themselves his yoke. The single yoke made perfect sense now. Yes, it was important for me to trust him and let him guide my way—to stop praying, "My will be done," and open my heart to, "Thy will be done." The easiest way to accomplish this is to listen to Jesus (particularly in the Gospels) and to follow his ways, which he tells us are easy and light. I am, once again, reminded that God does not ask the impossible.

Positive Vibes

Jesus is "the way and the truth and the life" (John 14:6); however, we are also told, "How narrow the gate and constricted the road that leads to life. And those who find it are few" (Matthew 7:13–14). Way to encourage us, St. Matthew! Instead of focusing on how narrow and difficult the way can clearly be—there's no arguing with that—I want to focus on how we can widen this road.

> *It can widen when we:*
>
> ☞ *accept that, despite all we have, without Christ we have nothing;*
>
> ☞ *open our hearts to experience Jesus, not just on Sundays for an hour but every day;*
>
> ☞ *share moments with Jesus in our everyday, ordinary life; and*
>
> ☞ *invite others to come and really know Jesus.*

Now Let Me Explain

First, it is easy to think that our lives are as good as they are going to get, especially if we have a comfortable life and enjoy good health. It is, also, easy to fall into a mindset of resignation if things aren't going well or we are not well, to chalk it up to that's how life is or to circumstances beyond our control. A faith in Jesus Christ is much more than a lucky charm or a wishing well; knowing Christ is making a new friend, one who has the words of wisdom to bring you hope, peace, joy, and love in every situation. How could you not want a friend like that?

Second, never assume that the person in the pew beside you or waiting outside the parish hall to pick up their children from religious education classes actually knows Christ as friend. I was a cradle Catholic who went to Mass almost regularly for ten years before I realized there was so much more to my Catholic faith than having a perfect attendance record to flash at the pearly gates.

The Catholic faith includes beautiful and powerful prayers (such as the Rosary, novenas, and litany of saints, just to name a few), an abundant gift of grace available in the sacraments (which offer healing in Reconciliation, strength in the Eucharist, and courage in Baptism and Confirmation, again, just to name a few), and the Scriptures, the Word of God, to guide my path and bring my dialogue with the Triune God to a whole new level. These are things no one told me or I somehow just missed along the way. I am grateful to have been blessed with people who cared to invite me to come and see, and once I did my life was transformed.

Taking upon myself the yoke of Jesus, I have learned, is not just one simple act. It is a series of discoveries and accepted invitations. For me, it was releasing the tight rein of control I insisted on having over my life. It was learning to trust in Jesus' teachings shared with me in prayer, the sacraments, and Scripture. The light and easy yoke is surrendering myself to the good that is the will of God for me and allowing Jesus to guide my steps and direct my path. The gift I give to myself is reading the Gospels, focusing on the wisdom of Jesus, and learning from the Master. The Master truly is the way, the truth, and the life—the life of peace, hope, joy, and love that I so desperately want for myself and for you.

An Invitation to Ponder

When you were reading about the exercise with the horse and Jesus, did you have a moment to picture yourself? Where were you? Where was Jesus? And, more importantly, who held the reins?

_____

_____

_____

_____

_____

_____

_____

_____

_____

_____

_____

_____

_____

Connecting to Scripture

PRAYER TO THE HOLY SPIRIT BEFORE READING SCRIPTURE

Come, Holy Spirit. Fill me with every grace and blessing necessary to understand the message, prepared for and awaiting me, in the

Scriptures. May I grow deeper in faith, in hope, and in love with Jesus as I spend this time with the Word of God. Amen.

✎ Psalm 94:19 _____

_____

_____

✎ Philippians 4:4-7 _____

_____

_____

✎ Mark 5:25-34 _____

_____

_____

✎ Mark 9:14-29 _____

_____

_____

✎ John 13:15 _____

_____

_____

John 14:25-29 _____

_____

_____

Romans 8:26-30 _____

_____

_____

1 Peter 2:21 _____

_____

_____

Scripture Reflection

Rest for my soul. Worry and anxiety leave my soul in a constant state of alertness. It is always teetering between fear and solace. It is a careful balance that I do not always maintain. I want to trust God. I try to focus on St. Faustina's words, "Jesus, I trust in you," but often, instead I say, "Jesus, I want to trust in you." I want, without that constant internal struggle, to believe that Jesus has it all under control. In those moments of trust, the peace is tremendous. When was the last time you felt that deep and abiding sense of peace? Has it been a long time? Do you, like me, have a balance of peace so delicate that even a feather of bad news or grain of doubt can knock it off kilter, allowing peace to escape from your heart?

The hope of lasting peace is the reason I accept Jesus' invitation to yoke myself to him. Experience has taught me that closeness to Jesus is the best antidote for the anxieties of this world. The times I keep my grace well filled by quenching my spiritual thirst with prayer, sacrament, and Scripture, I experience the peace that St. Paul explains as surpassing all understanding and guarding my heart and mind.

"When cares increase within me, your comfort gives me joy" (Psalm 94:19). The psalmist's reminder that the Lord consoles even my greatest worries, in itself, imparts great reassurance! Unfortunately, my first response to anxiety is not always prayer; usually, instead, I worry. For someone with anxiety, worry is an action verb. My response, then, is to try to control the situation through planning. Although this little gem from Proverbs, "The human heart plans the way, but the Lord directs the steps" (Proverbs 16:9), reminds me that the prayer plan is a much more fruitful idea. It is, also, a greater source of comfort than the old Yiddish proverb, "We plan, God laughs."

Control Freak Alert

My apologies before I make this next confession, as I know the Serenity Prayer and "Footprints in the Sand" are both Christian fan favorites. While I respect the reasons why people connect with these, I just never have. Maybe because both clearly abdicate control of your life, especially the difficult situations, to Jesus. This is something the control freak in me struggles with to accept the things I cannot change or to allow Jesus to carry me when I want the strength to always stand on my own two feet. The whole "holding onto the rein" visualization exercise from my retreat is probably making a lot more sense now! My need to be in control definitely steals the peace Jesus wants to give me.

Teresa of Avila is a credited with this comical story of her perception of how Jesus treats his friends. The legendary tale recounts a time when Teresa was traveling on the back of a donkey. During the trip, the donkey reared up, and Teresa was thrown into a mud puddle. It is said that while complaining of the circumstance to God, she heard him say that this was how he treated all his friends. She, then, pulled herself together, looked up to the heavens, shook her fist, and responded something to the effect of, "If this is how you treat your friends, no wonder you have so few of them."[6] Whether St. Teresa actually said this or not, the heart of this story expresses the way that many of us have surely felt at some point along our journeys with God. It really gets to the heart of the struggle I have with embracing a deeper relationship with Jesus. No matter how close I am with Jesus, he is going to allow me to fall into the occasional mud puddle. He'll be right there, and he will help me out of it, but he is not always going to prevent it from happening.

Bad Stuff Happens to Good People

How do we embrace a faith that preaches suffering at its core? Who wants to buy into that? My life has plenty of suffering, thank you very much. Bad things happen. Whether I like it or not, that is the way of this fallen world. There is no faith being preached that can change the outcome of the reality of being human. Bad stuff happens. The yoke that turns those burdens into light and momentary afflictions comes only from Jesus.

There is actually a promise that all will be worked together for good for those who love God. (Romans 8:28) Now that is balm for a weary and heavy-laden soul. All of this earthly stuff is temporary. Our pain is temporary. Our woes are temporary. Praise God for heaven because heaven is eternal.

Better Plans for You

In 2007, after several years of study, I had finally finished my master's degree in technology in education. Graduation brought me one step closer to realizing my dream of being a college professor. My alma mater contacted me about an opportunity to attend a weekend training so that I could be added to their roster of adjunct professors. I was beside myself with glee, especially after I was assured that I would have a course to teach in the new school year.

Assuming I had the summer free, I reached out to my pastor about facilitating a faith-sharing group for women. This was not something he had ever allowed before and took a great deal of preparation and heavenly intercession to get his approval. Small group faith sharing had transformed my life, and being able to provide this for the women in my parish was a great honor.

Then I received an unexpected voicemail from the college. A summer class had become available, and they wanted me to teach it. This was an amazing opportunity, the one I needed to get my foot in the door to realize my lifelong dream. I knew from the training sessions that if I could not accept a teaching assignment when it was offered, I should not expect another call, which is why I trembled as I heard the course dates listed in the message.

The course was scheduled to run on the same day of the week that I had chosen for the summer program at my parish. "How could this be?

Lord, how could you do this to me?" I prayed. The announcement for the faith-sharing group had already been announced in the bulletin, and from the difficulty I had just in getting a date, I knew there would be no rescheduling. Yet, if I didn't say yes to teaching this course, my dream of becoming a professor would essentially be over. I begged Jesus for some solution to this dilemma that allowed me to do both. The answer was clear and actually very surprising: if I were to follow what was on my heart, I would facilitate the small group faith sharing—which already had thirty participants signed up—and decline the teaching position. And that was the choice I made.

What seemed like the end of a dream was actually the Lord preparing me for an even bigger and, I would say, better dream. That summer, I fell in love with women's ministry and sharing the love of Scripture with others, and I discovered that I had a natural gift for sharing the faith. What I thought was the end of my dream was really the beginning of a new dream. In surrendering what I wanted for the plans God had for my life, a new dream emerged, which was more beautiful and bigger than I could have ever imagined.

Blessings abound in yielding what we want to what God wants for us. God only wants what is best for us; his will is always for our good. Even as I write these words, I wonder how often I've failed to see the good God was doing in my life because I was preoccupied with worrying about his plans. Peace comes when we're not at odds with God's will for our life, even if those plans include hardship and suffering. Instead of fighting our present trials, we can unite them to Christ's salvific work on the cross. We can offer all our prayers, praise, and work, along with our suffering, to him who perfects all. When we allow Jesus to guide our footsteps, when we take his yoke upon ourselves, not only does life become more bearable, but united with him, our praise, work, and, yes, even our suffering now has meaning.

An Invitation to Share

1. Which description of yoke best fits your relationship with Jesus? Do you need to allow him to guide your footsteps more? Do you need more time with Scripture so you can learn from him? Do you want to hitch up the double yoke so he can bear more of your heavy load? Briefly explain why you have chosen that particular description of *yoke*?

   _____

   _____

   _____

   _____

   _____

   _____

   _____

   _____

   _____

   _____

   _____

   _____

2. In addition to taking up Jesus' teaching, we are also instructed to take up our crosses. Each cross is perfectly sized for each of us, and when our crosses appear too big, we can be assured that God

will send us our own Simon of Cyrene to help us carry and bear the load of our crosses. What crosses are you currently taking up? Do they feel too heavy to burden alone? Whom has God sent to you to help you carry them?

_____

_____

_____

_____

_____

_____

_____

_____

_____

_____

3. Do you have a dream for your life? Have you brought your plans to Jesus in prayer? Have you experienced a change in your life plan or goals? Were you able to see God at work in these changes? What good did he bring?

_____

_____

_____

_____

_____

_____

_____

_____

_____

_____

_____

_____

_____

_____

_____

Closing Prayer

Lord Jesus, your invitation to take up your yoke is an incredible gift. How my heart fills with awe to see how your love for me extends into every aspect of my life! You genuinely care about my comings and my goings, my joys and my sorrows, my hopes and my dreams. This invitation conveys your yearning to see me grow ever closer to you and to adopt your model of faith as my own.

I am preparing my heart to learn from you and to follow your example of holiness. Renew your graces within me every day to embrace the peace only you can offer. My heart can be overcome by worry and doubt, especially when I lose sight of you in my daily life. Please bestow every grace and blessing needed to recognize that the plans God has for my life, family, and even our world are always for good. Let not my heart be troubled, but instead be reinforced with the knowledge of the sheer goodness of God's holy will. Lord, I desire to take up your yoke and enjoy the peace that is beyond all understanding.

The life you call me to is one that is overflowing with peace. Your yoke is easy, and with you my burdens are but momentary afflictions. Lord, thank you for these many incredible gifts; may I never take your generosity for granted. As I move forward in this study, please help me to see that every good and glorious gift comes from above. Help me to grasp the glory of your grace, how it impacts my daily life and fills me with joy beyond measure.

Dear Lord, be with me in my reading and reflection as I grow ever closer to you. Amen.

3: Invitation to Know the Gifts of God

Opening Prayer

Jesus, how grateful I am for the opportunity to have your grace envelop my heart and soul. This extraordinary gift of your Holy Spirit is undeserved yet freely bestowed upon me in the form of grace. You abundantly lavish it upon me when I seek you in prayer, sacrament, and in the Word. Who am I to be so loved by you?

Lord, please continue to help me respond to your loving nudges to come to know you better. Every day let me embrace the gift of being created to know, love, and serve you, in this world and evermore in the next. For so long I have hidden myself from you out of fear and insecurity, and I've often unsuccessfully tried to forge my own way. The fears and anxieties that remain in my heart have made it clear that this is not the path to true happiness. The joy of knowing you, my Lord, brings me strength and hope.

As I read this week's chapter, may I come to better understand the many gifts you have for me. I am eager to learn more about the gift of grace conveyed through time in prayer, reading the Scriptures, and participating in the sacraments. I realize how important grace must be in my pursuit

of faith and holiness when I consider that the Blessed Mother was filled with this gift. My heart is open and ready to receive all you have for me. Amen.

On My Heart

_____

_____

_____

_____

_____

_____

_____

_____

_____

_____

Invitation to Know the Gift of God

Gifts are really useful only if the recipient not only receives it but also opens and uses it. If a present remained unopened under the Christmas tree or in a drawer, it would be of little value. Certainly, the gift-giver would not have had that in mind when diligently searching for the perfect gift, spending her hard-earned money to purchase it, and then carefully wrapping this treasure. While the giver may be disappointed to see her gift go unused, the real loss in this scenario is to the receiver. Few people discard gifts, especially before they've even opened them, yet many of us do this with the extraordinary supernatural gifts bestowed upon us by God.

The Big Misunderstanding

When pondering unused gifts, I immediately think about the *Wii Fit* my sister gave me one Christmas. At first, I was a wee bit angry. While I am overweight and not a huge fan of exercise, she is thin and athletic. My immediate reaction to the gift, and all its body-sculpting accessories, was to perceive it as an insult. Although I may have received the present and removed the game from its wrappings, I did not ever intend to use it. How dare she, I thought, use Christmas as an occasion to tell me I was overweight.

After she left I shoved it and all the accoutrements into the closet. A few months later, my mother learned that her type 2 diabetes had worsened, and she was placed on daily insulin shots. A month after that, my father, who had had his first heart attack at thirty-four years old and a heart transplant at fifty-five, began a new battle with his health after a congestive heart failure diagnosis. Both of my parents' conditions, which may be inherited, are also conditions that can often be prevented by maintaining a proper diet and engaging in some type of exercise—exercise, perhaps, like the fun and low-impact *Wii Fit* my sweet baby sister had gifted me!

During a moment on the phone with my father as he discussed the medical procedures, medicines, and discomfort of this new health crisis that I realized that my sister's gift had nothing to do with physical appearance. She was not making a commentary on my size or shape. Her gift came solely from a place of immense love for me. This gift was to help me move my body and strengthen my heart, and, yes, she had hoped I would shed pounds because that would help me avoid diabetes. The gift was meant to give me a fighting chance to have a full, wonderful life, courtesy of a strong, healthy, and (hopefully) disease-free body!

So, What Are Your Intentions?

I misunderstood God's intentions in my life just as I had misunderstood my sister's intentions in giving me the *Wii Fit*. I looked at the Commandments and the "rules and regulations" of the Catholic Church, and I automatically assumed these had been put into place to tell me what to do. These, in my mind, did not come from a place of compassion but of oppression. Similar to the misinterpretation of my sister's gift, pride was blinding me from seeing the desire for my well-being overflowing in each of God's gifts. Faith, mercy, and, especially, grace are bestowed graciously, without cost from God for one simple reason: "God is love" (1 John 4:8).

God can be nothing other than love and loving in every action toward us. Everything he asks of us is ordered toward our good, toward our salvation, toward his desire to have us in heaven with him forever. His gifts provide us the means to have strong, healthy, and spiritually sin-free souls. His gifts are soul food, and we can consume as much of them as we want and never worry about becoming too fluffy.

In order for these magnificent graces to be effective in our lives, we need to be willing to receive, open, and use them. God is never outdone in his generosity. We are the fool-hearted who neglect to embrace all he offers to us. This is illustrated in the words from the Blessed Mother when she appeared to St. Catherine Laboure[7] and described the miraculous medal image. She explained that the rays emanating from her hands symbolize the grace abundantly available from God for all people. The bright rays that streamed from her fingers comprise all the graces God grants to people who are receptive to his amazing gifts. The dark rays represented the graces available but which remain unused. Grace is freely given, a total bargain. Since when have we stopped loving a bargain?

What Is Grace?

Most of my life was spent oblivious to the importance of grace. During that wonderful summer facilitating the faith sharing at my parish, one of the participants innocently asked me, "What is grace?" While I had a rudimentary understanding of grace, I could not formulate the appropriate words to express what I believed it to be. I realized at that awkward moment that I had no clue about what grace was.

That evening I dusted off my *Catechism of the Catholic Church* in search of some answers. "Grace is *favor*, the *free and undeserved help* that God gives us to respond to his call to become children of God, adoptive sons, partakers of the divine nature and of eternal life" (*Catechism,* 1996). The Allison-abridged version of the definition of grace is, "a freely given, yet completely undeserved, gift of God's Holy Spirit within us."

Furthermore, grace is:

☞ *UNMERITED—I can do nothing to earn it;*

☞ *FREELY GIVEN—it is a gift;*

☞ *GOD'S HOLY SPIRIT—now living within me;*

☞ *FOUND—when I seek it, and I do not have to look far; and*

*⌐ **ABUNDANTLY AVAILABLE**—particularly in the "grace trifecta" of prayer, sacrament, and Scripture.*

St. Thérèse of Lisieux, also known as "The Little Flower," asserted, "Everything is grace."[8] These are wise words from such a young saint. Since everything from God is grace, then everything from him is also gift.

The "Grace Trifecta"

Grace is freely given, yet completely undeserved. We cannot do anything to earn it; from his love we are lavishly gifted with the Spirit of God. Grace, though abundantly available, requires our willingness to allow God to touch our lives in this magnificent way. Grace helps us to choose holiness, including the help we often (okay, in my case, always) need to make the better choices that will continually lead us to God and to the holy lives he desires for us.

That summer over ten years ago, not only was I completely unsure of how to define grace, but I, also, had no idea how to seek an increase of it within myself. It was abundant and freely available; I could not earn it, but how could I open myself to receive it?

It would be many more years of studying Scripture and the *Catechism,* along with spending many hours in prayer and adoration, before my heart began to understand that best way to receive this abundant outpouring of grace was through what I affectionately refer to as the "grace trifecta."

This trifecta lays the foundation of a life of faith. It is found in our encounters with Jesus through prayer, sacrament, and Scripture.

Some Thoughts on Prayer

Prayer will be the topic of the next chapter, so I will just touch on one aspect of it here. After reading St. Paul's directive to "pray without ceasing" (1 Thessalonians 5:17), I started to look for simple, easy ways to incorporate prayer into my daily life. For me, this unceasing prayer does not mean I am on my knees or continually reciting a vocal prayer, but I am ever mindful of Jesus in my life. I am consciously aware that it is because of him that I have life. He is with me in all things and in all circumstances. My first prayer of the day is to ask for his outpouring of grace into my heart so that I may never forget any of the important lessons from my past nor miss out on any of the many blessings he has for me hidden in each day! If my first action of the day is to invite Jesus in and ask for his blessing on my day, maintaining awareness of Jesus in my life becomes far easier.

Participation in the Sacraments

At the core of every sacrament is an encounter with Jesus Christ (see *Catechism*, 1084-1090). It is impossible to have an encounter with Christ and not be changed. Every time we live out our baptismal promises, receive or adore him in the Eucharist, or seek forgiveness in the sacrament of Reconciliation, we are changed. One of my favorite aspects of the sacraments is how they interact with our senses. Catholicism is a full-body sport! In living a sacramental life we smell our prayers rising to heaven in the smoke of the incense; we see the body of Christ in the Church; we taste Christ's body and blood under the veil of bread and wine as we receive the Eucharist; we hear the call to holiness in the hymns, chants, and prayers; we feel the touch of Christ through his earthly representatives—priests—as they bless with chrism during a Baptism or Confirmation or anoint with oil as part of the Anointing of the Sick. The sacraments clearly bring us to our senses, and in doing so we are filled with amazing grace.

Scripture

"The Word became flesh *so that thus we might know God's love:* 'In this the love of God was made manifest among us, that God sent his only Son into the world, so that we might live through him.' For God so loved the world that he gave his only Son, that whoever believes in him should not perish but have eternal life." (*Catechism,* 458)

Scripture was the last element to be added to my "grace trifecta" idea. One day, as I pondered the role of Scripture in building a firm foundation of faith, an interesting equation came to me. I am not the best mathematician, but I have confidence in this little equation that helped me come to the conclusion that Scripture equals grace.

God gave us Jesus to redeem us out of love. Jesus is the Word made flesh. That Word is revealed in the Scriptures. Therefore, when we read the Word of God infused with his Spirit, we receive grace.

It is from a place of enormous love that God sends us his Holy Spirit to abide in us. That love manifests as an outpouring of his abundant grace. Therefore, reading the Scriptures opens our hearts and minds to the gift of grace. It is also an encounter with Jesus. It is impossible to have an encounter with Jesus, the Son of God, and remain the same. This is amazing grace.

An Invitation to Ponder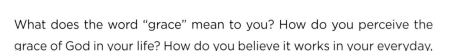

What does the word "grace" mean to you? How do you perceive the grace of God in your life? How do you believe it works in your everyday, ordinary life? Considering the three elements of the "grace trifecta," how can you personally take better advantage of the abundance of grace available to you?

_____

_____

_____

_____

_____

_____

_____

_____

_____

_____

_____

_____

_____

Connecting to Scripture

PRAYER TO THE HOLY SPIRIT BEFORE READING SCRIPTURE

Come, Holy Spirit. Fill me with every grace and blessing necessary to understand the message, prepared for and awaiting me, in the Scriptures. May I grow deeper in faith, in hope, and in love with Jesus as I spend this time with the Word of God. Amen.

✍ Psalm 84:10–12 _____

_____

_____

✍ Luke 6:46–49 _____

_____

_____

✍ John 4:10 _____

_____

_____

✍ Romans 5:15–17 _____

_____

_____

✍ Ephesians 2:4–10 _____

_____

_____

🖋 2 Corinthians 12:7-10_____

_____

_____

🖋 Hebrews 11:1-3 _____

_____

_____

🖋 James 1:12-17_____

_____

_____

Scripture Reflection

Christian music was actually my first foray into the psalms. I began listening to praise and worship music around the same time I began opening my Bible. I'd experience these amazing aha moments every time I opened and read the psalms. That is also when I discovered that most Christian musicians are plagiarizers! Although one cannot blame them because the psalms are filled with worship and praise. Psalm 84 is one filled with magnificent praise and worship lyrics gold. These verses in particular, bring joy to my heart:

Better one day in your courts than a thousand elsewhere.
Better the threshold of the house of my God than a home in
the tents of the wicked.
For a sun and shield is the LORD God, bestowing all grace
and glory.
The Lord withholds no good thing from those who walk
without reproach.
O LORD of hosts, blessed the man who trusts in you!

(Psalm 84:11–13)

One of grace's finest works is preparing our hearts to trust in the Lord. The gifts of the Lord are so bountiful. Faith is another of those glorious gifts. When I first learned that tidbit of information—that faith comes as a gift from God—was taken aback. Really, a gift? It is given freely by God, and with it we can receive all the other glorious blessings God has for us. How sad that few are willing to open that gift and use it to its fullest capacity. Cultivated faith grows receptivity to other important gifts, such as hope, mercy, and love. Living fully in the light of these incredible gifts, and so much more, is how we can glorify God.

My Hypocritical Faith

Sometimes the Word of God simply cracks me up. Aside from St. Paul's sweet greeting, "O stupid Galatians!" (Galatians 3:1), the verses that tickle me also cut right to the core of my not-so-stellar behavior. A case in point is the passage in Luke's Gospel in which Jesus says, "Why do you call me, 'Lord, Lord,' but not do what I command?" (Luke 6:46). Ouch, Big Guy. The lessons I've ignored the most frequently are usually the ones I've needed the most, and they are made easier to receive by availing myself of all the amazing ways grace is offered to me. God does not ask the impossible; in fact, each opportunity can be immensely enjoyed and can restore peace in one's life.

Praying is Easier Than You Think

When I was growing up, as I have shared, prayer was not presented as a routine (or enjoyable) activity. As a kid, my grandmother would always hand me a set of Rosary beads whenever I was homesick during my sleepovers at her house. Great idea, Gram, I used to think, by time I get even half way through this thing, I will be so bored, I will be fast asleep. Clearly, that is not what she had in mind. Now, as a faithful adult, I completely understand why she handed me those precious beads when I was afraid. She knew the power of prayer, especially prayer united with the intercession of the Blessed Mother. Not surprisingly, I always did fall asleep, but it was not because I was bored. Instead, covered in a mantle of prayer, peace would return to my worried soul, allowing me to rest.

Turning Self-Talk into Heavenly Conversations

For years, I talked to myself. I chatted a lot, but I never had anything really nice to say to myself. As I was learning to assimilate prayer into my everyday, ordinary life, I decided to make a conscious effort to transform my negative self-talk into encouraging conversations with people in heaven. Now, my internal conversations are with Jesus, Mary, my guardian angel, and whichever of my saint posse is best suited to my current situation. It has been life-changing and, I believe, responsible for the deep abiding faith I've been blessed to enjoy in my life.

Allowing the conversations to become natural did not happen overnight. I had to train myself to be more mindful of heaven by frequent participation in prayer, sacrament, and by reading Scripture. I discovered that this is where grace flows abundantly and profoundly.

Prayer, sacrament, and Scripture each offers in its own way a tremendous outpouring of grace into our lives. Grace readies our hearts to hear what God has to say, and to receive this grace, we have only to ask. Grace helps us believe in hope that "whatever you ask for in prayer with faith, you will receive" (Matthew 21:22), but this doesn't mean you need a mountain of faith; God can work with our mustard seed of faith (Luke 17:6). The mustard seed is a teeny tiny seed that blooms into one of the largest bushes.

When we offer Jesus even the smallest piece of our hearts, it comes back to us bloomed beyond our expectations. God is never outdone in his generosity. St James writes, "Draw near to God, and he will draw near to you" (James 4:8). St. Mark includes Jesus' teaching, "Therefore I tell you, all that you ask for in prayer, believe that you will receive it and it shall be yours" (Mark 11:24). In her diary, Polish nun and mystic St. Faustina shares these words from Jesus, "At three o'clock, implore My mercy, especially for sinners; and, if only for a brief moment, immerse yourself in My Passion, particularly in My abandonment at the moment of agony. This is the hour of great mercy. In this hour, I will refuse nothing to the soul that makes a request of Me in virtue of My Passion."[9]

These are all tremendous promises, however, unless we make time to seek a relationship with Jesus made possible by grace, we may never witness them in action in our own lives.

An Invitation to Share

1. Consider the three elements of the "grace trifecta": prayer, sacrament, and Scripture. Which do you feel you have the least difficulty participating in? Which do you feel is the most difficult to make time for? Share one way that you can begin to implement each element this week to allow more of the gift of God's grace to flow in your life.

_____

_____

_____

_____

_____

_____

_____

_____

_____

_____

_____

2. What has been one of your favorite gifts that you have received? From whom did it come from? Did this gift change your life in any way? If so, how?

_____

_____

_____

_____

_____

_____

_____

_____

_____

3. If it were possible to wrap up and gift anything in the world (not necessarily an object, it could be an idea, virtue, or feeling), what would you give? To whom would you give it?

_____

_____

_____

_____

_____

_____

_____

_____

_____

_____

_____

Closing Prayer

Word of God, speak to my heart. May I read the Scriptures as a guide to my life and be constantly aware that in them I will find you, my Lord. I continue to strive to take your yoke upon me and learn from you.

You teach me through the Scriptures, and I hang on every word in the Gospels. However, my heart is not always confident that I am living out your teachings as you desire. Each day I will begin by beseeching you to guide and teach me.

I need your grace, your Holy Spirit, to live within me, to inspire me, to understand what it is you are teaching me in Word, prayer, and sacrament. I want you to continue encouraging me to persevere when I don't understand or when I am frightened by circumstances in my life or the world around me. Your Word is light and true life. My life, until now, has been lived according to my own ideas and attempts to conform to what the world has asked.

Every day I see how unfathomable you are. I can never plumb the depths of all you wish for me, and I now realize how little I have embraced the life to which you have called me. I am overjoyed at the prospect of the more time I spend in prayer, sacrament, and Scripture, the closer we will become. As my life has unfolded with its trials and tribulations, and as I've buckled beneath those burdens, you watched eagerly and waited for me to turn to you. I now long to live a life alongside you, ever seeking to be filled with grace, to give you my heart, and to give back through using all the gifts that you have given me.

Dear Lord, be with me in my reading and reflection as I grow ever closer to you. Amen.

4: Invitation to Ask in His Name

INVITATION

Opening Prayer

Jesus, I come before you with my hopes and dreams tucked in the deepest recesses of my heart. Some days, I am apprehensive about bringing them before you, fearful that your plans for me may not include fulfilling these hopes and dreams as I perceive them. The difficulty of accepting the fact that not every dream presented in prayer will be a part of your divine will is eased with your gracious invitation to ask anything in your holy name.

Prayer seems so easy; how hard can it be to have a conversation with a friend? However, when that friend also happens to be the Son of God, the belief that my words are actually heard runs smack into the doubt lurking deep within my soul. The truth is, Jesus, you would not invite me into this intimate relationship along with your promise of receiving and responding to my cries if you were not inclined to do so. My heart is filled with hope as I cling to your pledge to hear and answer me, especially in my darkest moments.

I delight in the relationship prayer builds between you and me, Lord. Who am I that you should care for me? Who am I to come before the throne of grace, confident that my prayers reach your ears and move your heart? Timidly, humbly, and awestruck by your majesty, I come to this chapter seeking to grow ever closer to you by accepting your invitation to encounter you in prayer. What I ask first in your holy name is simply to never lose my faith and hope in you. Amen.

On My Heart

Invitation to Ask in His Name

It is so easy to grow weary in prayer especially when it doesn't appear that our prayers are being answered. Jesus teaches us to be persistent and to persevere in prayer; I'm going to go out on a limb here and guess that since he takes the time to teach about it, the problem is not unique to me.

My biggest crisis of faith, and losing the desire to pray, came after two devastating losses. My first son, Ian, was born two months early but, gratefully, very healthy. Although tiny, within two weeks of his birth he was home with us. Fifteen months later I was pregnant again and overjoyed to be expanding our little family. However, a few weeks into the pregnancy, I knew something was not right. The pregnancy was ectopic; it required emergency surgery and nearly took my life. A year later, I became pregnant again, only to lose that baby in a miscarriage. After losing my second child, I was done with praying. Why bother? Either God wasn't listening to me anymore, I clearly didn't know how to pray properly, or maybe God was just a figment of my imagination. Each scenario gave me little reason to persevere in prayer.

I Just Couldn't Stay Away

Interestingly, after a short time of trying with all my might not to pray, I just couldn't stop myself from having conversations with my heavenly family. Before the pregnancy losses, I primarily prayed for things. My prayers were only petitions. This experience revealed the naivety I had about how prayer worked. Prayer is not telling God what to do, but rather it is raising our hearts and hopes to him. There are many other kinds of prayer, including praise, thanksgiving, and intercession. I had to learn the difficult lesson that we don't pray to get our wishes grant- ed; we pray because it opens our hearts and minds to a spiritual life with God. What a gift we've been given to enjoy this grand privilege of communicating with heaven. After I lost the babies, I realized that I needed to keep praying because I needed comfort, and my heart longed to praise God for sparing my life so I could be here to care for my son Ian.

I had reopened the line of communication with the Father, Jesus, the Blessed Mother, the holy souls in purgatory, and my saint posse—the particular saints on whose intercession I call most often. (My saint posse changes as my life evolves, but primarily the group consists of Saints Thérèse and Faustina, Blessed Solanus Casey and Stanley Rother, Venerable Patrick Peyton, my guardian angel, and the Blessed Mother.) Now the next step was to genuinely learn to entrust all my prayers to God's holy, compassionate, and perfect will, and not allow disappointment to keep me from praying, either for myself or for others.

Praying for Others

One of the greatest honors for me is being asked to pray for someone. People are quick to call upon me during difficult or dire circumstances. My heart absolutely breaks when the prayer request is not answered in the way we had hoped. I misguidedly feel that I have failed at my task or let my friends or family down when the sick person passes away, the job is not landed, or the much-desired baby is not conceived or lost to miscarriage.

Prayer does not work like the genie's lantern. We cannot just say the magic words and have a wish granted. That is just not how faith in God works. He answers our prayers according to his will and for our good. There is such a tendency to want to stop praying when you feel like you're not doing it right or when the situation never seems to be affected by our prayers until we realize one very important thing explained painstakingly clearly by the prophet Isaiah:

> For my thoughts are not your thoughts,
>   nor are your ways my ways—oracle of the LORD.
> For as the heavens are higher than the earth,
>   so are my ways higher than your ways,
>   my thoughts higher than your thoughts. (Isaiah 55:8–9)

May I Pray for You?

To my delight, my friends, family, and even strangers continue to come to me for prayer, regardless of the outcome of previous petitions. The experience of being sought to pray, especially after your last prayers went seemingly unanswered, teaches me that the fruit of prayer has nothing to do with me. It is not about me or even about you; it is all about grace.

Effective prayer is not about the result we see but about the peace we feel. I believe Jesus' greatest response to our supplications is with an outpouring of his peace. "Peace I leave with you; my peace I give to you. Not as the world gives do I give it to you. Do not let your hearts be troubled or afraid" (John 14:27). The repeat prayer requesters in my life, mean the world to me not only because I find such joy in praying for others but also because their requests illustrate the power of intercessory prayer. In Jesus' name we pray, and from that prayer, whatever it is, peace will abound.

Prayer properly disposes our hearts to accept the will of God; through prayer flows every grace and blessing we need to keep our hearts from being troubled. The very first Scripture verse I memorized was Philippians 4:6–7[10]. Still today, this verse is among my favorites and is one of the most repeated throughout my day. St. Paul invites us to pray about everything and worry about nothing; to tell God everything we need, with a thankful heart, and welcome a peace that surpasses all of our understanding. This extraordinary peace, St. Paul's advice concludes, will guard our hearts and minds in Christ Jesus.

Sometimes that peace is hard for me to grasp no matter how much I pray. I live with a great deal of anxiety. If you could medal in worrying, I would have a gold. I have worried since I was a little kid; remember,

I had the mother who seemed to pray with us only in cases of emergency, like severe thunderstorms, and that left a lasting impression.

Ave Maria

One of the most harrowing experiences of my life occurred during World Youth Day in 2013 in Rio de Janeiro. We were leaving Copacabana Beach after the opening ceremony Mass. People covered the beach from the water's edge to the access road. Literally millions of people were trying to exit this narrow strip of beach. We were being pushed and shoved and squished; I was sure I was going to be trampled to death right there on the beach. At only five feet, three inches tall, I was armpit height, and every backpack pressed against my mid-section. The more the crowds pushed in, the harder it became for me to breathe. I had to use all my strength to make a space to turn sideways to let air into my lungs.

As the crowd pressed in, my immediate reaction was to begin praying out loud to the Blessed Mother. "Ave Maria," I repeated over and over. This was not a natural prayer for me, yet the words flowed easily and, to my surprise, rather loudly. In hindsight, this prayer choice made perfect sense. "Ave Maria" would have been understood by most of the pilgrims around me, regardless of the language each spoke. Perhaps our Blessed Mother had put it on my heart to speak out loud like that, in a manner uncharacteristic of me, to bring peace to those who were frightened around me as well. Sometimes our prayers are not spoken words or even conscious thoughts but, rather, are just a cry in the dark for help from heaven. It was horrifying, and I didn't understand why the Lord had brought us there just to allow us to be killed. Well, clearly he didn't let me die that day. Gratefully, no one died exiting the beach that evening. The next morning at Mass, as I knelt to say my prayers before the service began, I was overcome with fear. That terrifying experience happened on only the first night; there were so many nights to come, and I couldn't imagine putting myself through an experience like that again.

I said to the Lord in my distress, "Why would you bring me here just to give me such a frightening experience? Why would you put me in such grave danger?" Jesus responded to me with such gentleness. He quieted my fears with, "Allison, you say that you love and believe in me, but yet you fear meeting me. You must stop looking at death as a punishment and realize it is a reward.

Prayer is not how we manipulate God or the circumstances of our lives; it is how we accept and understand what God has for us. He does not bring the bad, but if he allows it, he has a greater good that he will bring from it. That idea is so hard to understand it doesn't seem right. Why would a loving God allow us to suffer?

Pick Up Your Cross

A few years later I believe the Lord gave me an interesting insight into his call to pick up our crosses. It came during a time I was presenting Confirmation retreats in my area. Sadly, I have discovered it is generally difficult to teach teenagers about the Catholic faith during a retreat they feel they were forced to attend. Recognizing this hurdle, it became my mission to make these Saturday or Sunday afternoons as personally beneficial and as interactive as possible. At one particular retreat, there was a young man who was ready to argue with me—on everything. As the end of the retreat drew near, I sensed he was getting agitated as his behavior grew disruptive. When he realized that the priest, the parent volunteers from his parish, and the director of education were absent from the auditorium, he saw and seized his opportunity to set me and my teachings straight. This fifteen-year-old boy—still dressed in a suit after having volunteered at a funeral—stood up, looked me straight in the eye, and proceeded to tell me to get over myself, sprinkling in some lovely profanity for good measure.

In the heat of the moment, I made the biggest mistake of my retreat-leading career. Instead of diffusing the situation, I decided to enter into battle with this young man, feeling totally convinced that I could teach him to see how awesome God and, more importantly, the Catholic Church really are. My very flawed plan was to dazzle him with my brilliant explanations until he admitted how wrong he was. In the most horrific moment of my entire teaching career, the plan backfired. The harder I tried to defend God and his teachings, the worse the situation became. He had an argument for everything, and I quickly concluded that I was ill-equipped for defending the faith against his misunderstandings and biases. Everything spiraled down and out of control. I had teens crying and running out of the room. Recalling the moment makes my heart ache. Plainly speaking, it was a fiasco.

At the end of the horrible day, I got into my car, and I began driving home. I called my student teacher and bawled. She told me to get to a church as quickly as I could to spend some time with Jesus. Best advice ever. I went to my parish because I knew it was open and the chapel was always available. I sank into the pew, looked upon the tabernacle with Jesus within it, and began to cry even harder. Through my tears I said out loud, "Lord I don't understand this. I do everything that you ask. I gave up my career in order to follow you and share how awesome you are, I go to Mass; I pray; I spend time in adoration; I'm following all of the rules and responding to what I think you're asking. Yet here I am, crushed by this experience with an ill-mannered teenager. I've failed so very miserably, Lord."

As I sat forlorn in the church, the Spirit presented these powerful truths:

- *If God did not spare his Son, what makes you think you'd be any different?*

- *If you want to share in God's glory, you must be willing to share in the suffering.*

- *If you want to follow Jesus, truly follow him, you must pick up your cross—daily.*

Praying and offering these difficult moments to the God who needs nothing unleashes a tenfold return of his grace and blessings upon us. It is not about changing his mind or convincing him to act according to our will. "Prayer is the raising of one's mind and heart to God or the requesting of good things from God," an invitation to bring ourselves humbly before heaven (*Catechism*, 2559). To ask of the Father, in the most precious name of Jesus, is another magnificent gift from God.

Invitation to Ponder

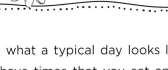

Take a few moments to reflect on what a typical day looks like for you. When do you pray? Do you have times that you set apart, to purposefully pray without interruption? Have you found ways to pray "without ceasing" throughout your day, as St. Paul encouraged us to do? In what ways do you usually pray?

_____

_____

_____

_____

_____

_____

_____

_____

_____

_____

_____

_____

_____

_____

Connecting to Scripture

PRAYER TO THE HOLY SPIRIT BEFORE READING SCRIPTURE

Come, Holy Spirit. Fill me with every grace and blessing necessary to understand the message, prepared for and awaiting me, in the Scriptures. May I grow deeper in faith, in hope, and in love with Jesus as I spend this time with the Word of God. Amen.

Psalm 37:3-5 _____

_____

_____

⌐ Matthew 6:9–13 _____

_____

_____

⌐ John 16:23–24 _____

_____

_____

⌐ Ephesians 6:10–20 _____

_____

_____

⌐ Hebrews 4:12 _____

_____

_____

⌐ 2 Timothy 3:14–17 _____

_____

_____

Scripture Reflection

What a beautiful thought, to simply delight in the Lord and know he longs to give me the desires of my heart. Now, if I only knew what those desires were. Some might be obvious: meaningful work, a loving spouse, maybe to have children or a nice home. What else could these desires be? Can these desires of my heart, spoken of in Psalm 37, always be put into words and expressed to ourselves, to others, or, most importantly, to God?

Even if I recognized the longings within myself, I would lack the words to adequately express them. St. Paul writes, "The Spirit too comes to the aid of our weakness; for we do not know how to pray as we ought, but the Spirit itself intercedes with inexpressible groanings" (Romans 8:26). The desires God has fulfilled in my life were not longings I had been conscious of until they had been satisfied.

The fulfillment of one such longing came with the adoption of my daughter, Faith. We adopted Faith from China, and she is profoundly deaf. Her journey into our family was, without a doubt, a "God thing." Adoption had never entered into any conversations I had had with my husband, Kevin, and we actually spent almost seven years without any children. Before I rediscovered Jesus, I was too busy and, honestly, too insecure to become a mother. But by the grace of God, we were blessed with two boys. Though the road to motherhood was wrought with hardships, including two heartbreaking miscarriages, we were content with the family God had blessed us with after seventeen years of marriage. Then to our surprise, during a Stephen Curtis Chapman concert, we began to have our hearts stirred for adoption.

Where did this idea come from? It was so strong that we knew it was from God, and we knew "resistance is futile."[11] Shortly after beginning the adoption process, I had a conversation with my mother. She was not at all surprised by our decision to adopt. She recalled a memory from my elementary school days when I blurted out, rather matter-of-factly, that when I grew up, I was going to not only going to adopt but specifically adopt children whom others may not want to adopt. The desire was placed on my heart by God, and it lay in wait until the perfect time for God to bring it to light.

But Wait, There's More

The conversation with my mother continued, and this was when the Holy Spirit really knocked my socks off. In addition to that early declaration of mine, she vividly remembered another afternoon from my middle school days. I had come home from an after-school program in which I had been learning American Sign Language. I told my mother I wanted to have a deaf child when I grew up. She recalled giving me the most baffled look and explaining that it didn't really work that way, that you couldn't choose to give birth to a child with a hearing loss. Furthermore, she was confused about why I would wish for my child to be born deaf.

Good question, Mom. I wondered that too, why I had actually continued to desire to mother a child who was deaf. Was it just the beautiful language? I could certainly learn that without having a deaf daughter? It was not until after reading Psalm 37 that it all started to make more sense.

Could it be that this seemingly bizarre desire for a child who communicated through American Sign Language and the passion to adopt a child who might wait a long time for an adoptive family were placed on my heart by God so that when he called me to go to China and bring Faithy home, I would say yes?

Yes, I truly believe so. I, also, believe this wonderful experience may not have ever occurred if I hadn't been prepared to listen to the promptings of the Holy Spirit to follow my heart created through my time in prayer. Even though I had not been specifically praying for that intention, the Spirit had interceded, and this mission that had been put on my heart, as inconceivable as it seems, had become a reality. Our God is truly an awesome God![12]

Prayer Is a Powerful Weapon

The armor of God is a powerful image St. Paul paints for us in his letter to the Ephesians. Do you have this spiritual armor at your ready? Are you clothed in truth and righteousness? Do you hold up the shield of faith, knowing as the Veggie Tales say, "God is bigger than the Boogie Man"?[13] Faith is a formidable weapon against the evil that prowls the earth looking to devour our souls, the evil that threatens daily to paralyze us with fear or steal our salvation with its lies. Brandish the sword of the Word of God with boldness because it is a gift unlike any other. The Scriptures are God's Word—the living, dynamic, mighty Word of God. Rewind and take a moment to read those words again, slowly. It is an incredible, mind-blowing truth. The God of the Universe, the unseen God, the deity we sometimes struggle to believe in because we cannot see his face (this side of glory), allows us to hear him.

Prayer raises our hearts to God, and the Scriptures fill our hearts with assurances of love, hope, and mercy. This is just a glimpse of the mystical stuff of the Catholic faith that makes it so magnificent, and is all the more reason to make time for reading the Scriptures, even if all you have time for is one verse, even one word. The grace that flows from allowing the Word to speak into heart and soul can sustain your connection with God throughout your entire day.

No Book Like the Good Book

There is absolutely no other book on any of my shelves that I can pick up every single day and be inspired by. These inspirations are more than simply feeling good after I read, like a typical good book. The Scriptures teach me, encourage me, and spur me to live out what I've just read. They are truly a living, dynamic, endless source of spiritual nourishment.

For our part, we must make time to hear. When I was first integrating daily prayer and Scripture reading into my day, I literally put it on my calendar. I called it, "Coffee with Christ," and like any other appointment on that calendar, I made every effort to keep it!

Jesus models slipping away from the din and demands of the world and finding silence in your life. How often I have thought, well that was easy for him to do. He didn't have to attend to kids who needed help with homework or who were involved in a million after-school activities while still working, cleaning the house, and getting supper on the table; he didn't have a boss with unreasonable demands and ridiculous deadlines; he didn't have sick parents who needed assistance or to be cared for. However, that does not mean he is unsympathetic to those challenges in our lives. Jesus understands our afflictions and our infirmities; he is empathetic to our human weaknesses. So we can bring these challenges to him, ask for his help to find those quiet moments with him, and trust that his grace will make a way.

God is the Creator; we are the creations. I know I often forget that, especially because I work in ministry, and I mistake us as coworkers sometimes. I'm sure that makes him giggle because he is clearly The Boss. Not the kind of boss who wants to push me around, but the kind of boss who wants to see me succeed, who wants to give me every support I need to do the best job I can do, to be the best in whatever I have been created to be. St. Catherine of Siena is credited with wisely saying, "If you are what you should be, you will set the whole world on fire!"[14]

Our lives should be lived to glorify God, to seek him and his will for us in all things. He promises us every grace and blessing we need to realize the desires he has put upon our hearts. We merely need to take our mustard seed of faith and boldly ask in the name of Jesus.

An Invitation to Share

1. Do you struggle to see the effectiveness of your prayers? Have you experienced a time when your prayers felt empty or unanswered? If so, how did you push through it? If you are there now, how can the lessons of this chapter help you to rejuvenate your prayer life?

_____

_____

_____

_____

_____

_____

_____

_____

_____

_____

2. How familiar are you with the Bible? How has spending these last few weeks reading and reflecting on it impacted your prayer life? Do you feel any more attuned to Jesus in your life?

_____

_____

_____

_____

_____

_____

_____

_____

_____

_____

_____

3. Which desire of your heart do you feel God has delighted in giving to you? Which desires do you believe are yet unsatisfied? How can you discern which ideas and thoughts come from you and which are placed there by God? What have the Scriptures from this chapter shown you that can help with that discernment?

_____

_____

_____

_____

_____

_____

_____

_____

_____

_____

_____

_____

Closing Prayer

Jesus, thank you for allowing me to hear your voice in my life through your Word. Thank you for the many amazing gifts you have bestowed upon me.

What a sweet and loving Savior you are to speak so clearly and gently to me through your Word and into my heart during times of prayer. You are near to me always. My uncertainty at opening your Word has slowly been replaced by an excitement to spend more time with you through it. What a gift you offer me, Lord, in your invitation to spend time in prayer and to boldly approach the throne of grace with my petitions made in your holy name.

May the Holy Spirit continue to move and stir my heart to desire to spend this time with you every day, even if just for a few moments. May this time together enlighten my heart with hope in the darkness, with encouragement in my despair, and with peace in all my tribulations.

Help me to turn to you in the joys of my day as your Word has opened a new door to a relationship with you. I can learn to listen in the everyday, ordinary circumstances of my life. I can turn to you for guidance in making everyday decisions and for the ability to feel your love, so that when the storms come, my firm foundation will have been built.

As we continue to learn of your invitation to be loved by you, may that love, which is illustrated again and again in your Word, melt my heart and make me receptive to new experiences with you.

Dear Lord, be with me in my reading and reflection as I grow ever closer to you. Amen.

5: Invitation to Forgive from Your Heart

INVITATION

Opening Prayer

Jesus, please send an outpouring of your grace upon me that I may learn to more easily offer forgiveness, as well as to accept forgiveness. The hardest act of forgiveness, Lord, seems to be, sadly, toward myself. You lavish your mercy upon me, but I often show none to myself. Lord, help me to know the healing power of being reconciled to you. Guide my heart to fully embrace your gift of healing mercy in even my most grievous offenses, for there is nothing you cannot forgive.

In this chapter, dear Lord, may I begin to recognize the importance of letting go of the past—all those situations that still cause me so much pain despite the time that has passed away. Lord, how I desire to accept your invitation to forgive from my heart, not only others but myself as well. Bring me along the path of peace to which forgiveness and mercy lead me.

Forgiving is an act of the will, a divine action, and I am not able to accomplish it without the grace of God. Teach me how to forgive others from my heart, so my heart will be prepared to receive forgiveness from you, my Lord and Savior. Strengthen me to embrace the joy and peace inherent in forgiving both others and, especially, myself. The heart of the Gospel is forgiveness. May this chapter inspire me in your love to follow your glorious example. Amen.

On My Heart

_____

_____

_____

_____

_____

_____

_____

_____

_____

_____

_____

_____

_____

_____

_____

_____

Invitation to Forgive from Your Heart

The sacrament of Reconciliation changed my life forever. Discovering the power and grace that flows from a sacramental confession transformed my pain into peace. The mercy shown to me by Jesus in this sacrament has continued to change my life every time I have participated in it over the course or more than ten years. Bitterness and disappointments from my childhood, numerous missteps while I navigated adulthood, and the loss of important relationships along the way have left me battered, bruised, and often fighting depression and on the verge of despair. Gratefully, God in his wisdom provides this great gift to free us from burdens like those.

The sacrament of Reconciliation, also known as the sacrament of Conversion, the sacrament of Penance, and the sacrament of Confession, offers me something nothing else in this world does: the gift of hearing the words of absolution spoken to me, "Your sins are forgiven" (*Catechism,* 1484). It is a gift to sit face-to-face with the priest, who comes in the place of Christ, or in persona Christi, which the Catechism explains as follows:

> In the ecclesial service of the ordained minister, it is Christ himself who is present to his Church as Head of his Body, Shepherd of his flock, high priest of the redemptive sacrifice, Teacher of Truth. This is what the Church means by saying that the priest, by virtue of the sacrament of Holy Orders, acts *in persona Christi Capitis:*
>
> > It is the same priest, Christ Jesus, whose sacred person his minister truly represents. Now the minister, by reason of the sacerdotal consecration which he has received, is truly made like to the high priest and possesses the authority to act in the power and place of the person of Christ himself (*virtute ac persona ipsius Christi*).
>
> > Christ is the source of all priesthood: the priest of the old law was a figure of Christ, and the priest of the new law acts in the person of Christ. (*Catechism,* 1548)

The presence of a person acting on behalf of Jesus in the confessional allows us to hear with our ears the glorious words of absolution. You are forgiven. There is no guessing or wondering, just the relief of having our sins washed away by love and mercy.

Reconciliation is a sacrament of healing, just as Anointing of the Sick is. It was discovering this classification that surprised me the most, but makes perfect sense! I am overjoyed that the information did not elude me forever because I have come to truly understand that the mercy of God is his greatest gift.

Bring Your Broken Places

Jesus patiently awaits the day when we invite him into our broken places so he may heal them through his merciful love. As he mends, he extends an invitation to us to share our burdens with him, to submit into his loving care all those dark, dingy places deep within us that only he can fix. Sometimes in prayer, I visualize the pain I am bringing to Jesus as a tired old room. I imagine Jesus patiently emptying the room, cleaning the cobwebs and dust, and then performing a spiritual remodel through an outpouring of his love and grace.

As the Master Carpenter, he can make over any interior brokenness into useful grace. As the Great Physician, Jesus can truly heal every ailing dream, hope, and emotion, whether you are broken emotionally, physically, financially, socially, or spiritually. I have some scars of my own in every one of those areas of my life, and I have seen Jesus work miracles in them all. If you allow him to enter, he can mend, heal, and even transform your broken places too.

He Just Wants to Love You

Above all things, Jesus just wants to love you. For me, accepting his mercy and love were closely tied together, and I struggled to feel worthy to receive both. Although no one is worthy on their own merit to receive these astonishing gifts, through our adoption as beloved children of God the Father Almighty, we are made worthy. However, knowing these are freely given gifts bestowed from above and allowing myself to receive, open, and use them are completely different responses.

After sharing this interior struggle with a wise priest, he thoughtfully challenged me to articulate how I allowed Jesus to love me. As I pondered this question, I realized my difficulty stemmed not particularly to Jesus, as Lord and Savior, but to God, as Father. I couldn't accept the love of the Son because I had yet to accept the love of the One who sent him. Father Joe instructed me to sit with this question for a while and quietly contemplate my relationship with God. He suggested that I not only think about how love is shown but also pray for the Spirit to reveal it, and, perhaps, even use this as an opportunity to visualize how I am loved by God.

The next day, I nestled into the window seat in my bedroom. I sat there for a long time staring at the sky, unable to envision how God showers (or even sprinkles) his love upon me. I felt sad as I realized that what I had developed over the years was a distant and an almost fear-based belief in him. At that time in my life, I could honestly say I did not know what it meant to be loved by God. The tears fell softly down my cheeks as, through my prayers, I began searching in earnest for some reference point where he and I could begin to connect. I prayed, "God, I want to feel your love, but I do not know what it looks like."

Suddenly, I recalled one of my favorite childhood memories. On Sunday afternoons, my dad and I would curl up on the couch to watch

NASCAR racing. This Sunday cuddle time with my dad was precious because my dad worked nights which prevented me from seeing him during the week. As this sweet memory washed over me, I started to understand better how God loved me. His love was not found in the spectacular, but more often he loved me in the midst of the ordinary, everyday, simple moments of my life. As my heart swelled with this newfound understanding of the Father's love for me, I was interrupted by my children seeking a snack and some cuddles of their own. After tending to their needs along with myriad other daily responsibilities, I was eventually able to return to my window seat and revisit the fruitful and very powerful visualization exercise.

That time when I sat in the window seat staring at the sky for answers, it did not take long to revisit that sweet memory of being curled up, content and secure, with my dad. That quickness of reconnection taught me something I hadn't expected: God's love is always there; he is always there. Even when I have been swallowed by the distractions of the world, he is there. What it means to be loved by God is to be content in the knowledge you are never alone. You are treasured every moment of your life by our Heavenly Father, who loves us perfectly, without conditions or caveats. While at first it had taken me so long to let down my guard and to truly let God love me, once I had experienced this love, it did not take me more than a moment to recognize it during our next encounter. God is there, always patiently waiting for us to receive and rest in his amazing love.

Maybe you are struggling to recall special memories or moments with your own father with which to compare the love of God the Father. After many years of women's ministry, I hope it is of some comfort to you to know you are not alone in that struggle. However, allowing God to love you will not only help erase the pain the absence of this relationship may be causing you but also provide you with the opportunity to heal through forgiveness. Forgiveness is actually an important step in opening your heart to experience the love of God. A heart filled with bitterness, anger, and resentment is not free to love. So, when are you going to start allowing God to love you?

Mercy through the Sacrament of Reconciliation

Offering mercy, especially in the sacrament of Reconciliation, is yet another incredible way God demonstrates his love. The following passage from the *Catechism* is one of my favorite explanations of the peace and joy that comes from participating in Confession:

Reconciliation with God is thus the purpose and effect of this sacrament. For those who receive the sacrament of Penance with contrite heart and religious disposition, reconciliation "is usually followed by peace and serenity of conscience with strong spiritual consolation." Indeed the sacrament of Reconciliation with God brings about a true "spiritual resurrection," restoration of the dignity and blessings of the life of the children of God, of which the most precious is friendship with God (*Catechism,* 1468).

The grace I received from the sacrament of Reconciliation was healing my wounds. The bitter roots I'd cultivated during years of holding onto every hurt had grown very deep. The gift of reconciliation was curing what had vexed my soul for so long and eliminating what had kept me from building a relationship with God, Jesus, the Holy Spirit, and every other friend in heaven available to assist me in my journey heavenward. Through my inability to forgive, I had hardened my heart without being attentive to the spiritual consequences. Bitterness, I once read, is the pill we swallow in hopes that the other person will suffer. In reality, when we refuse to let go of the hurt and anger weighing on our hearts, the suffering only truly affects us.

Overcoming Being a Confession Chicken

So why should we go to Confession? First, we recognize the transformative power of the sacrament as described in the Catechism:

> Interior repentance is a radical reorientation of our whole life, a return, a conversion to God with all our heart, an end of sin, a turning away from evil, with repugnance toward the evil actions we have committed. At the same time it entails the desire and resolution to change one's life, with hope in God's mercy and trust in the help of his grace. This conversion of heart is accompanied by a salutary pain and sadness which the Fathers called a*nimi cruciatus* (affliction of spirit) and *compunctio cordis* (repentance of heart). (*Catechism,* 1431)

A "radical orientation" of my life is pretty powerful language for this crazy practice of walking into a little room with a priest, whom you may or may not know, and spilling your (sometimes long) laundry list of the things you should not have done and the things you have failed to do. To many people it seems ridiculous that we cannot simply express their contrition to the Big Guy ourselves. Why do we even need a middleman?

Here are my thoughts on the beauty and blessing of the sacrament of Reconciliation from my converted confession-chicken heart!

Petrified, would be the best word to describe how I approached Confession as a second grader before my first Holy Communion, as a teenager before Confirmation, as a young adult before my wedding, and as a slightly more mature adult following my reversion back to the Catholic Church—and every other time in between. My heart raced, my palms sweat, my throat closed, and my feet wanted to sprint to the nearest exit. Honestly, I hated every moment of it, until

Jesus made me laugh, and the Holy Spirit provided a little insight into the gift of that so-called middleman.

Jesus Made Me Laugh, Hysterically

We were just a week or two into attending our new parish, and I was very excited for my first Confession there. I was glad not only because the confessional had one of those privacy screens but also because I had not been at the parish long enough for the priest to recognize my voice. Although at this point in my spiritual journey I would still consider myself a confession chicken, I was eager and excited for my nearly anonymous confession. I was first in line. One of my tricks for conquering my fear was to go early so there would not be any (or many) people waiting for Confessions before me.

That Saturday afternoon, I entered the confessional and closed the skinny door behind me. The booth was small with a well-worn kneeler; face-to-face confession was not an option. I quickly jumped in to my confession with, "Forgive me, Father. It has been [way too long] since my last confession, and here are my sins." I had managed to share a few items from the list I brought in with me (yes, I actually write them down) when the priest interjected from the other side of the screen, "Excuse me, but are you the woman who has come to start the new youth group?" *What? Um, well. Ugh, I was. Now what?*

In that awkward moment, I felt like I had two options: one, I could lie and then start back my confession with, "I lied one time just now to you"; or two, I could go the more sensible route, own up to the fact I clearly have a very recognizable voice (I refuse to believe those screens don't actually hide my identity), and just continue on with the rest of my confession. However, that is not what happened. After I admitted that I was, indeed, the new youth group leader, he went into a ten-minute soliloquy on all the fun and exciting ideas he had for us to explore. I finally got up the courage to interrupt and ask if we could return to the confession. He readily agreed, and I continued with my list.

When I finished, I had been in there for a good fifteen minutes, and because it was a Saturday, there were a good number of people waiting. I had just thanked Father for his time, opened the door, and made eye contact with some of the now ten or so people waiting their turn when I heard, "Oh, one more thing." *Wait? What is happening? Is he really calling me back into the confessional?*

Unsure of what to do, I broke eye contact with the people waiting to come in, the people who were now staring at me frozen in the doorway. I sheepishly closed the door and knelt back down. I am fairly certain that half of the people sitting and waiting for their turn in the confessional bolted for the door. I mean, really, who gets called back into Confession? The half who remained all had to add to their sin list: "I judged one time that lady who was just recalled to the confessional"!

This sweet, eager priest wanted to tell me all about the marriage retreat that he was involved with and that he thought my husband and I would enjoy! Finally, after another ten or fifteen minutes, I was free to go and complete my penance.

After inquiring with the priest about the existence of, perhaps, a back exit or trap door—thought maybe he could just drop me secretly and safely out of this embarrassing situation—I reluctantly opened the door and made my way to the pew to complete my penance. As I knelt to pray, the hilarity of what had just occurred washed over me, and I burst into laughter. If anyone had observed me from behind, I would have appeared to have been hysterically crying; however, I was actually making a valiant effort to stop myself from hysterically laughing. In that moment, I had been overcome with an understanding I had never grasped before: that time in the sacrament of Reconciliation is an encounter with Christ, the true Christ, and he obviously has an incredible sense of humor!

The Spirit's Insights

The physical nature of our beings, at least mine, seeks physical experiences. The remarkable gift of speaking with a priest in Confession is one I nearly threw away because I did not understand what God was offering to me. I had a fear of stepping into a confessional and facing a priest, but I also had doubts about the purpose and necessity of Reconciliation. Since I was likely to commit (most of) those same sins again, why should I bother confessing them? What was the purpose of going to Confession when I'd just be back again with the same junk? I didn't understand that the grace poured out through the sacrament of Reconciliation could help me the next time I was faced with similar temptations. Cooperation with grace comes with the Spirit's assistance when faced with the opportunity to not choose that same sin again or, at least, to not choose it as quickly as I had the last time.

The daily examen, which "is a technique of prayerful reflection on the events of the day in order to detect God's presence and to discern his direction for us," is wonderful[15]; it is an important check-in with Jesus daily about where we met or failed to meet the challenges of each day. Saint Ignatius suggested we do it twice a day. And you should absolutely have this conversation with God whenever you feel you have sinned to let him into your heart and show your contrition. But the real gift comes from being face-to-face with the priest. When we allow Jesus to wipe our sins away with the words from the priest who is there in persona Christi. There's no guessing whether you're forgiven because you actually hear the words of absolution. In that moment, all of your sins are forgiven. Confession is not just an obligation or duty, it is so much more than that! It's not a meaningless rule the Church imposes upon us, but, rather, it is a great gift—yes, another gift that God has for us.

Celebrating Forgiveness

Sure, we probably will slip back into some of the behaviors we just resolved to turn away from, but even the tiniest bit of change is still conversion. Confession is an encounter with Jesus. Every encounter with Jesus transforms us; we are never the same person after spending time in prayer, receiving the sacraments, or reading Scripture. His mercy heals and strengthens you, and restores your joy. The feeling that comes from allowing his grace to pour into your heart is glorious. As a long time religious education teacher, I have witnessed many second graders warily walk from the pew to the confessional for their first Penance. Their strides are slow and labored, and their shoulders droop. They look back a few times, hoping for a change in plans and to be called back to the pew. Yet, when they emerge from the confessional just a few moments later, they are skipping and dancing, high-fiving their friends, all the way back to their seat in the pew.

God wants you to feel that joy every time you experience Reconciliation, and he doesn't want you to wait a year or two or more between each visit to the sacrament. We are called to confess our sins at least once a year according to the precepts of the Catholic Church. But confession should be so much more than an obligation. It should be an opportunity to rid ourselves of our burdens and accept the grace that God has for us. Even a minuscule amount of grace helps us continue moving forward. It is still a mending of that brokenness. You may have to return to the sacrament again and again for a regluing of sorts, but each time those pieces mend the bond is stronger. Eventually the situation becomes so covered in sacramental grace that it holds together. God is the Master Sculptor. We are God's workmanship. "For human beings this is impossible, but for God all things are possible" (Matthew 19:26).

Because we have received the astounding gift of the sacrament of Reconciliation, we do not need to remain in the shattered pieces of sin and shame; we can come to his mercy and be made whole again. He's come to give us life and to give it to us abundantly (John 10:10). His work on the cross opened heaven and provided us with this amazing gift of mercy. The heart of the Gospel is forgiveness. As with the gift of grace, we are only hurting ourselves if we leave this gift of Reconciliation unopened and unused.

An Invitation to Ponder

What thoughts and feelings does the word "forgive" invoke in your heart? When you think about showing someone mercy, how does that look to you? What is your idea of God's mercy? Contemplate how his mercy is so vastly different from the human understanding of mercy. Does that make it easier or more difficult for you to experience God's mercy in your own life?

_____

_____

_____

_____

_____

_____

_____

_____

_____

_____

_____

_____

_____

_____

_____

_____

Connecting to Scripture

PRAYER TO THE HOLY SPIRIT BEFORE READING SCRIPTURE

Come, Holy Spirit. Fill me with every grace and blessing necessary to understand the message, prepared for and awaiting me, in the Scriptures. May I grow deeper in faith, in hope, and in love with Jesus as I spend this time with the Word of God. Amen.

Psalm 51:3–12 _____

_____

_____

✐ Matthew 18:21–35 _____

_____

_____

✐ Luke 6:31 _____

_____

_____

✐ Luke 15:11–32 _____

_____

_____

✐ John 10:10 _____

_____

_____

✐ 2 Corinthians 5:18–20 _____

_____

_____

✐ Ephesians 4:31–32 _____

_____

_____

Scripture Reflection

Ironically, this was the most difficult chapter for me to complete. Since 2009, I have been reading and learning about peace and sharing that peace offered through forgiveness. After experiencing the devastating loss of several close friendships, I realized my ability to forgive or to ask for forgiveness was seriously lacking. My past hurts, even those going way beyond those of friendships, had left me stuck in place that had stolen my peace. As I discovered the freedom of forgiveness offered through Christ in the Scriptures, my heart began to heal and peace reigned once more. That process and monumental discovery led me to launch my ministry, Reconciled To You.

Perhaps the struggle to write this chapter came from trying to condense all the amazing insights I've been blessed to obtain over the years. When we can forgive others from our heart, all the pain, bitterness, and resentments are replaced with peace that truly does surpass all understanding. Forgiveness was at the core of Jesus' salvific work. His mercy, freely given, like grace, is a gift we cannot afford not to receive, open, and use.

Unforgiving Servant

Probably my biggest misconception about forgiving was in believing that forgiveness was a feeling. It is actually a choice, a deliberate decision. I first learned this when I discovered the book, *Forgiveness: The Catholic Approach,* which, in my opinion, is one of the greatest books ever written on forgiveness. This one sentence, "It's a decision because by forgiving we choose to let go of any desire for revenge or retaliation, and we free ourselves of the bitterness and resentment that harden our hearts,"[16] changed my approach to forgiveness, forever.

Before I truly understood forgiveness, my feelings alternated between anger and sadness. I kept anticipating that one day I would just wake up and feel different, that somehow I could make myself feel those emotions less, which would equate to "being over it." Yet, while I waited for that feeling to come, I would rehash conversations we had, rehearse possible future encounters, and endlessly second-guess both past and possible future decisions. I was refusing to let go of the hurt, thereby imprisoning myself within despair, and I was continuing to replay the past situations over and over in my mind, further ensuring that I would never be free from the pain.

After living this way for a while, I came to accept that state of existence. Even though I was miserable, I was comfortable in that misery because I knew what to expect. My bitterness and I had become very close, and the longer we hung out together, the more unlikely the possibility of being free of it became. We were cozy—bitterness, anger, sadness and I. We had become best buddies! It never occurred to me to consider forgiveness—that seemed like giving in, or letting those who hurt me off the hook. Nope, forgiveness was neither an option nor a necessity, not yet anyway. I justified holding onto all of these resentments until I reached the day when I would feel something inside myself signal that I was ready to forgive.

Any doubt that I was called to forgive immediately was dispelled when I read the parable of the unforgiving servant in Matthew's gospel (Matthew 18:21–35). That was a serious game changer. Whatever offense I have committed against God outweighs any offense that anyone could ever commit against me, and yet God always forgives. If he were able to forgive my great debt, I could certainly find it within myself to forgive lesser debts against me. If

I could not, this self-imposed imprisonment had the potential to become far more permanent.

Forgiving is a difficult task, but God never asks the impossible. Here again, grace is the answer. Forgiveness requires the grace of God to be accomplished. As Paul said, "I have the strength for everything through him who empowers me," (Philippians 4:13), and when we ask for this grace to overcome even the longest standing hurts, he will grant it. This is true of the hurts we hold against ourselves as well as against others.

The Hardest One to Forgive

Inevitably, when I give a retreat on the topic of forgiveness, women will share how they struggle to forgive themselves. Mothers lament parenting decisions. Adult children regret broken or strained relationships with parents (living or deceased). I realized as I spoke with other women that I was not the only one who gets stuck and replays the same scenarios over and over again in my head: things I said that I wished I hadn't said; things I didn't say that I so wish I had; decisions with unexpected outcomes that can't be taken back; the pain of lost jobs, severed friendships, and more all coupled with the anxiety of our inability to change the past. "Do not worry about tomorrow; tomorrow will take care of itself. Sufficient for a day is its own evil" (Matthew 6:34). This is true of the past as well. Sing it with me, "Let it go, let it go."[17]

Furthermore, we are taught by Jesus to treat others as we would want to be treated. That has a completely different spin on it when you are so merciless toward yourself. If you are like me, you are much quicker to forgive others for their mistakes, lack of judgment, or poor decisions before you let yourself off the hook for the same behavior.

In Matthew's Gospel, Jesus instructs, "You shall love your neighbor as yourself" (Matthew 22:39). Sometimes I think, I'm good with this one because I usually like my neighbor more than myself. That is not exactly following his teaching; we are missing the important *I* there. We are to love others and ourselves, if for no other reason than that we have been created in the image and likeness of God, and as my grandma used to say, "God don't make junk."

Parable of the Lost Brother

Luke's Gospel contains a parable you are probably familiar with—the prodigal son. Maybe it was just me, or did you also miss that the parable includes a disgruntled brother?

He said to his father in reply, "Look, all these years I served you and not once did I disobey your orders; yet you never gave me even a young goat to feast on with my friends. But when your son returns who swallowed up your property with prostitutes, for him you slaughter the fattened calf." He said to him, "My son, you are here with me always; everything I have is yours. But now we must celebrate and rejoice, because your brother was dead and has come to life again; he was lost and has been found." (Luke 15:29–32)

I can totally relate to the brother's issue, though not necessarily with respect to my siblings but to the world in general. While I have been no angel, especially as an adolescent, I felt that, for the most part, I followed what God asked of me. I tried to be good person, to be helpful and kind, and to keep the Commandments. When hurt by others I would seethe as good things continued to happen to them while I wallowed in my anger, bitterness, and resentment. I would rail against God: "How could you let them just get away with that Lord? You saw what they did." The thing is, not only did he not miss the exchange between you and that person, but he also sees into that person's heart.

He knows their motives and their intentions. He loves them as much as he loves you, and wills the good for them as well as you. It is a misconception to believe someone is getting away with hurting another; likewise, it is constraining God to our human perception to feel slighted when he welcomes our offender back into his loving embrace.

The Scriptures guide our hearts in this as well: "Beloved, do not look for revenge but leave room for the wrath; for it is written, 'Vengeance is mine, I will repay, says the Lord'" (Romans 12:19). God misses nothing. All of us are accountable for our actions, as we say in the Confiteor, "in what [we] have done and in what [we] have failed to do." In fact, our response should always be to pray for our enemies that they not receive their just punishment. Not only is that healing and the Christian response to being hurt, but it is also what we should hope is being done for us. No one wants to be judged according to what we have coming. God's love, and, gratefully, his mercy are sufficient enough for each and every one of us.

The father in the parable comes out to the pouting brother in the field; he meets the brother where he is. The father lovingly explains how everything is still available for him, that just because he is generous with one child does not mean he takes away from another. The parable ends before we learn of the brother's response. Can he accept the father's conditions and rejoice along with him, or does he insist on justice his way and remain in the cold? What decision would you make?

It Is Good for You

The most unexpected benefit from forgiving another is the freedom, joy, and relief it brings to your whole being. The reaction of your body, mind, and soul to the hurt and pain you are holding onto may not even be something you are consciously aware of, but, believe me, it is there.

As Hurd notes in his book *Forgiveness: The Catholic Approach,* "recent scientific studies confirm the healing power of forgiveness. They conclude that people who forgive live longer, healthier, and happier lives." Furthermore, he reminds us, "we deny ourselves the gift of God's forgiveness (which is foolishness to us)," and "the abundant life Jesus invites us to share."[18]

As a kid I suffered from awful stomach issues, and I had every test in the medical books. No one could determine the cause, and years—and many therapists—later it became obvious that I had made myself physically ill by trying to hold in feelings and emotions. I was too young to put words to what I was feeling or why, but it was clear that my body was relying upon itself to handle everything. The chosen coping mechanism was neither healthy nor helpful. Therapy definitely helped to begin revealing the source of that pain, but the roots remained for a long time. They would recede for a bit, but then a word, event, or image would bring them all rushing back. Pope St. John Paul II wrote, "The liberating encounter with forgiveness can be experience even by a wounded heart, thanks to the healing power of God, who is love."[19] Since St. John Paul II forgave Mehmet Ali Agca, the man who attempted to assassinate him, I hold his thoughts on forgiveness in rather high regard.

Until I had discovered God's mercy, I continued trying to internalize and suppress negative feelings towards others instead of face them or bring them to God, and I had made myself physically ill. Being introduced to the precious knowledge that there was an alternative and walking this struggle with Jesus was life changing. I had a safe outlet, and his abundant grace, to forgive and be free.

My initial coping mechanism was neither healthy nor helpful, but then I discovered the healing available in the sacrament of Reconciliation. I could try all I wanted to force myself to forgive, but without God's grace, I was not going to accomplish it. In Confession, my healing didn't come just from dumping all my "junk" on the priest; instead, it was from handing all my burdens over to Jesus. I was laying them at the foot of the cross. I was emptying myself of the guilt, shame, pain, and bitterness, and into that empty place God was pouring in *his* Holy Spirit—*his* Grace. Grace is the undeserved, yet freely given, gift of God's Spirit, his Holy Spirit, within us. That gift of grace provides what we lack in our flawed human form: true forgiveness.

A Place to Find Healing

Forgiving and being able to move on didn't happen overnight. In most instances, it required several visits to the sacrament of Reconciliation to work through the tangle of what my responsibility was in the situation. In the sacraments, we encounter Christ. In every encounter with Jesus, we are transformed, maybe only a little at a time, but each time we pray, read Scripture, or participate in the sacraments, we are forever changed. Jesus came "so that they [we] might have life and have it more abundantly" (John 10:10). A heart filled with bitterness, malice, and rage is not capable of living an abundant life. It is indeed liberating to let God transform your heart and to open yourself to experience forgiveness.

In Second Corinthians, we find one of my favorite verses. It is actually the one on which I based my entire ministry, to promote reconciliation with God through prayer, sacrament, and Scripture; and most importantly to be an "ambassador for Christ" (2 Corinthians 5:20).

> And all this is from God, who has reconciled us to himself through Christ and given us the ministry of reconciliation, namely, God was reconciling the world to himself in Christ, not counting their trespasses against them and entrusting to us the message of reconciliation. So we are ambassadors for

Christ, as if God were appealing through us. We implore you on behalf of Christ, be reconciled to God. (2 Corinthians 5:18–20)

In the end, we have only one choice. To adhere to St. Paul's exhortation to put aside all bitterness, anger, resentment, and forgive others as God has forgiven you in Christ. Remember above all else, God never asks the impossible. If he calls you to it, he will provide you with every blessing and grace to accomplish it.

An Invitation to Share

1. In John's Gospel, we learn that Jesus came to give us abundant life. How do you see Jesus fulfilling that in your own life? Do you take full advantage of the gift of his mercy so that you can live in the freedom that comes with the life he came to give you?

2. Whom do you best relate to, the prodigal son or his brother? Why?

_____

_____

_____

_____

_____

_____

_____

_____

_____

_____

3. Do you have someone in your life you need to forgive? What keeps you from offering this forgiveness? Is this someone you wish to be reconciled with? Does knowing that you can forgive without ever telling that person or reconciling with them make it easier to work with the grace of God and to let go of the bitterness, anger, or pain? Do you find it as easy to forgive yourself as it is to forgive others?

_____

_____

_____

_____

Closing Prayer

My initial reaction to seeing my sins is to hide. Run from them. Embarrassed and ashamed, I don't want to admit my sins. I don't want to admit that I have hurt you, Lord, and I don't like to relive those sinful moments again and again. So I avoid—or, rather, I avoided— Confession, Lord, not realizing that in it, you had more in store. You had healing in store for me. All those moments that I have tried to lock myself away from you in the dark recesses of my mind, actually convinced that I could keep them from you. Hidden, they have done me no good, and in the darkness they only became bigger lies and burdens. That is not how you want me to live. You did not die upon the cross for me to live in this darkness. Lord, you have come to give me peace and an abundant life. You have come to bring me mercy and forgiveness. This week, I thank you, Lord, for opening my heart to accept that mercy and forgiveness, to be more willing to seek you and the sacrament of Reconciliation, to know that you are calling me in there only to free me and not to embarrass me. When I speak those sins out loud, I am bringing them into the light, where your love, mercy, and grace can shine upon them, dispelling the darkness.

Confession is not meant to be an exercise in shame or humiliation, but to be an opportunity for healing. Renewed and reconciled, I can go forth to know and love you even better. In Confession, I am brought back into right relationship with God. I return to you with all my heart. The gift you have given me is having somebody to hear my confession and respond audibly with the words of absolution so that I may never guess whether I have been forgiven. What a gift the grace of forgiveness and mercy truly is.

Help me to be more courageous this week and in the weeks to come to make frequent visits to the sacrament of Reconciliation so that I can continue to heal and grow in faith. Thank you for this great gift of forgiveness, healing, and hope. Immerse me in every grace I need to overcome my fears of receiving this great sacrament. Renew my spirit, and create a clean heart in me.

Dear Lord, be with me in my reading and reflection as I grow ever closer to you. Amen.

6: Invitation to Believe in Him

INVITATION

Opening Prayer

Jesus, I pray with all my heart that I will accept your invitation to a deeper communion with you. Through reception of the Eucharist, I am blessed to be closer to you than even the men and women who walked beside you in Nazareth, Galilee, and Jerusalem. Your institution of the Eucharist at the Last Supper, the giving of your own body and blood, is something I will never fully comprehend, yet I pray for the grace to receive the wondrous gift you have offered. The magnitude of this gift is beyond human intellect, so I approach the Eucharist with faith like a child, accepting that this is truly you offered in Holy Communion.

Awed, Lord. I am awed by your majesty. I am humbled that you would offer me this incredible gift of receiving the bread of life and the cup of everlasting life. My senses are, indeed, feeble, and I can only marvel at the magnitude of this gift. I long to be like St. Peter, who knew that only you have the words of eternal life. May your Spirit enlighten my heart that I may look upon the host, which confounds so many in its appearance of a wafer, and believe beyond any shadow of a doubt that it is you—body, blood, soul, and divinity.

May the great gift of the Eucharist, along with all the signs and wonders shown upon the earth, help me to develop an even stronger faith in you. Lord, I long to believe without proof, but my senses fail me often, and my confidence wanes. Have pity on me, and help me in my unbelief. Jesus, I trust in you. Amen.

On My Heart

_____

_____

_____

_____

_____

_____

_____

_____

_____

_____

_____

_____

_____

Invitation to Believe in Him

Although I was raised Catholic, many aspects of the faith remain a mystery to me. Every day I feel like I learn something new about the deep, rich traditions of the Catholic Church. It really is amazing! The plethora of devotions and practices of faith available astonishes me.

It is impossible to plumb the depths of all that Christianity has to offer for that would be trying to completely contain and describe an unfathomable God.

A fruitful tradition I have uncovered as I have learned more about the Catholic faith has been adoration of the Blessed Sacrament: the practice of visiting a church or chapel while the Eucharist is displayed upon the altar within a monstrance. We come, as the wise men (magi) and shepherds did over two thousand years ago, to adore Jesus. This practice of spending time with Jesus in adoration started enriching my faith life quite serendipitously, as some might say, over ten years ago. But after many hours spent praying in his presence, I would say this had the Holy Spirit's fingerprints all over it!

My husband and I, along with our children, had just made the transition to a new parish, which was not completely unfamiliar to us, as Kevin and I had met and were married there. After our wedding, however, we had moved out of town and spent many years attending my childhood church, where we remained until my original Bible study friends left the Church. The memories, both of the good times and now the sad, eventually became too painful, and I knew I needed to find a new place to call our spiritual home. That is how we arrived at this new, old parish, where I would be introduced to someone who would become one of the most significant influences on my spiritual life.

I was going through a very difficult time spiritually, emotionally, and mentally. In hope of accelerating the healing of my bruised heart, I decided to attend Mass at least once during the week. I knew the extra time with Jesus in the Eucharist would bring me much needed grace for my current trial. One morning after daily Mass, Mrs. P., the mother of my high school bestie and the person whom I would describe as the "seed planter" of my faith, was sitting and chatting with a friend on the little stone wall right outside the lower church's doorway.

She looked up to greet me with a smile and the warmth that I rarely encountered anywhere else. After exchanging pleasantries, she inquired about whether I had signed up for an hour during the parish's weekly Eucharistic adoration held on Saturdays. I felt a little embarrassed as I didn't know much about Eucharistic adoration, and I definitely had no desire to spend an entire hour sitting by myself in the musty chapel on a Saturday afternoon.

The Blessing of Adoration

What happened next, though I would not realize it until many years later, was about to change my life—forever. That may sound a bit dramatic, but it is the truth. Mrs. P. explained that she was responsible for assuring that Jesus, present in the Eucharist and displayed in the monstrance on the altar, was never left unattended during Saturday adoration. She explained there were a few time slots left to be filled and asked if I would consider helping out.

Saturday? Are you kidding me? Really? The only time adoration is offered is on Saturday?

At the time, I had two young children heavily involved with soccer and baseball, plus Saturdays were set aside for housework and errands. There was no way that I could give up any time on a Saturday, but that look in her eyes said I wasn't being excused until I had, at least, looked over the schedule. My plan was simple: out of respect for her I would take a peek at the sign-up sheet, then quietly leave (possibly through the other exit), without having committed.

Back into the chapel I went. I looked over the sheet, found no time available that worked for me, and waited for what I thought should have been enough time for her to have finished visiting with the other woman. Confident that she would be gone, I emerged from the chapel. And there she was. *Drat!* "So," she asked, "did you find time to spend with the Lord?" *How am I going to get out of this?* I quickly pondered. "No Ma'am," I responded (not exactly the brilliant escape plan I had hoped for).

She gently encouraged me to go look again. "I am sure there is an hour you can give to Jesus," she said, sounding just like Jesus in the garden at Gethsemane with his three sleepy disciples (Luke 22:45-46). Obediently, I marched back in and stared at the only empty line on the schedule of adorers—2:30 to 3:30 p.m.

Really, Jesus? The middle of the day on Saturday? This is all you have for me? Ugh. You are not making this easy.

So without signing my name in that inconvenient slot, I headed back out of the church. I thought that, surely, Mrs. P. had left by now, except I was wrong—she was still there!

Undeniably, she was a messenger from the Holy Spirit that day, and, gratefully, neither of them were accepting *no* for an answer! I went back and signed up for 2:30-3:30 p.m. At the time, I had convinced myself that I'd keep the commitment for a few weeks and then erase my name. Well, as it turned out, I could not have been more wrong. I kept that hour, diligently and happily, for three years! Eventually, we discovered a quaint little church, closer to our home and in our diocese, which lead us to consider changing parishes again. The deciding factor in this new move was the availability of adoration of the Blessed Sacrament every weekday. A direct gift of God's grace, if you ask me, for my humble obedience in making time with him so many years ago. Over ten years later, the blessings from keeping at least one hour a week with the Lord have become too numerous for me to count.

The Need for Signs and Wonders

Having Jesus present in the Eucharist is one of the ways the Lord helps me to see him. Like Thomas, I need to touch and see. In one sense, I believe I am beholding Jesus with my eyes in the real presence of the Eucharist. However, I would be lying if I did not admit that there is a part of me that struggles with this reality as I look upon what appears to be ordinary bread and wine. I am called to see with eyes of faith, where, as St. Thomas Aquinas says, "the feeble senses fail."[20]

I'm the first to admit that I act a bit spoiled when it comes to how often I ask God to prove he is at work in my life. By the very fact that he is God and I am not, I have absolutely no right to ask him to prove himself. However, I am overwhelmed daily by his generosity in constantly doing just that. As it was for Thomas the Apostle, believing what I cannot see is a challenge. These little glimpses of God, which I dub "godcidences," are special opportunities for me to develop keener eyes of faith. Faith, according to the author of Hebrews, is "the realization of what is hoped for and evidence of things not seen" (Hebrews 11:1). Each of these miraculous moments—modern day signs and wonders—are so lovingly provided strengthens my relationship with Jesus is strenghened.

One such occasion occurred not too long ago. I was on my way to adoration, and I knew my constant fears and anxieties were overwhelming me and putting a wedge between myself and the peace Jesus has for me. I had become acutely aware that my fear of being sick, having a debilitating injury, and, even worse, dying was dominating my thoughts. These fears were paralyzing me and keeping me from doing the things that I believed the Lord wanted me to do. Having just gone to Confession the night before, I knew that these fears were teetering on serious sin. I was in danger of slipping into despair instead of trusting in the Lord. While driving to the chapel, I brought all these concerns to Jesus in prayer. I didn't specifically ask for a sign to help put these fears to rest, but I did beg for his mercy in this area of my life.

I had once read something by Venerable Father Patrick Peyton, in which he spoke of the great power of praying the Rosary before the Blessed Sacrament. Oddly, despite my love of the Rosary, it was not one of my normal holy hour activities. However, on this particular day, as soon as I settled into my pew in the chapel, I pulled out my rosary beads and began to recite the prayers. After a few decades, I had an overwhelming sense of peace and comfort in my heart, along with this crazy notion to text my friend the screenshot of the butterfly I had discovered on Facebook earlier in the day.

Butterflies had become very special to her and to me over the last few years, although for very different reasons. We each see them as sweet reminders of God's immense love for and care of us. For my friend, the butterfly brought comfort as she suffered from a devastating loss, and for me they became a significant sign of hope during the adoption of my daughter, Faith. As I prayed, the nudge to send the butterfly image became too strong to ignore. I actually looked at the Eucharist nestled in the middle of the beautiful Monstrance and teasingly said to Jesus, "Dude, aren't we kind of in the middle of something here?" I chuckled to myself and obeyed because I just knew it was something I was not to ignore. So I fished my phone out from the deep recesses of my purse and quickly sent the picture to my friend and added that I was praying for her.

Within seconds she wrote back and shared that my timing was perfect because it was the fourth anniversary of her father's passing. In fact, until she had seen the butterfly, she had totally forgotten the significance of that day. I was overwhelmed with the sense of how much God loves his children. He had not only answered my prayer for peace and the understanding that there is something not to be feared beyond this world, but he had also given this great, unexpected gift to my friend. Through my tears I typed back, "You are so very welcome. And, PS, heaven is real."

While my spiritual goal is to believe without these sweet reminders from above, I am so very grateful for the spoiling. Each instance is a powerful reminder that God cares intimately for me. My kind-hearted spiritual director, Deacon Jerry Ryan, always prays over me at the end of our sessions. Recently, his prayer summed up my relationship with signs and wonders and the state of my faith. "Lord, in your loving mercy," he prayed, "please continue to shower this woman with butterflies, roses, and Fidelity trucks because she clearly needs them." My weakness is made perfect in his grace. When it comes to accepting Jesus' invitation to believe in him, how blessed am I that he chooses occasionally to bestow grace outwardly. "But blessed are your eyes, because they see, and your ears, because they hear. Amen, I say to you, many prophets and righteous people longed to see what you see but did not see it, and to hear what you hear but did not hear it" (Matthew 13:16–17).

An Invitation to Ponder

Can you recall a time in your life when a coincidence really may have been a "godcidence," a time when the circumstances were a part of heaven reaching out to assure you in your faith? While signs are not meant to be talismans, nor are we to become reliant on them to believe in God, does something in particular always make you think of God or heaven?

_____

_____

_____

_____

_____

_____

_____

_____

_____

_____

_____

_____

Connecting to Scripture

PRAYER TO THE HOLY SPIRIT BEFORE READING SCRIPTURE

Come, Holy Spirit. Fill me with every grace and blessing necessary to understand the message, prepared for and awaiting me, in the Scriptures. May I grow deeper in faith, in hope, and in love with Jesus as I spend this time with the Word of God. Amen.

Joshua 24:17 _____

_____

_____

Matthew 26:36-46 _____

_____

_____

Mark 9:23-24 _____

_____

_____

John 6:52-69 _____

_____

_____

John 20:24-30 _____

_____

_____

1 Corinthians 11:23-26 _____

_____

_____

Scripture Reflection

In Baptism, we receive an outpouring of the gift of faith. We become the adopted daughters of God the Father. Our work, however, is not finished with this sacrament of initiation. Baptism is only the beginning; we are called to continue to grow in our Christian life through participation in it. Faith is a gift that needs to be used in order to be cultivated. Learning about your faith is critical to understanding it. For instance, I needed to learn that the Eucharist was truly Jesus' body, blood, soul, and divinity (*Catechism,* 1374 and 1413). Sadly, I had been incorrectly taught that it was only a symbol.

After reading chapter 6 in John's Gospel, it became quite clear that the Eucharist is not a symbol. Jesus proclaims that "unless you eat the flesh of the Son of Man and drink his blood, you do not have life within you" (John 6:53). Many disciples around him mumbled at the difficulty of his teaching and a great multitude of them even abandoned him. Instead of yelling after the throngs leaving, "Hey, wait! Let me explain," Jesus turns to Peter and the other disciples and asks, "Do you also want to leave?" (John 6:67) If Jesus had meant for this consumption to be symbolic, he would have quickly clarified it as he had done in so many other situations. Based on all we know about Jesus as teacher prior to this point in the Gospel, we can confidently deduce that if his teaching was being misunderstood, he would have called them back and explained. The fact that he does not further solidifies the truth that, "my flesh is true food, and my blood is true drink" (John 6:55). Of the true presence of Jesus in the veil of bread and wine, St. Thomas Aquinas said that it "cannot be apprehended by senses, but *only by faith*" (*Catechism,* 1381).

If You Can

Often my prayer resembles these words spoken in Mark's Gospel by the father of a boy who has come to beg the Lord to heal his son: "But if you can do anything, have compassion on us and help us" (Mark 9:22); and then, "I do believe, help my unbelief!" (Mark 9:24) I do believe and I trust that Jesus can help, usually, but part of me always wrestles with a complete surrender. One reason why I love the sacraments is that they are outward signs of God's efficacious grace (*Catechism,* 1131). Sadly, as I have already admitted, I am a woman of little faith who craves signs and wonders to help me believe. On more than one occasion, the Holy Spirit has guided me to Jesus' gentle chastisement in the Scriptures where he says, "Unless you people see signs and wonders, you will not believe" (John 4:48). Yet, I still seek them, and, gratefully, he still sends them.

The Rosary Walk and the Fidelity Truck

In 2015, as my husband prepared to begin his first classes in the diaconate formation program, I was struggling with mysterious ailments, my father-in-law's health was on a steady decline, and my children were each working through some challenging situations in their lives. I knew I needed to do something monumental to shore up the walls of our home and of our hearts.

My usual response to situations requiring big prayer is to offer a novena. Nine days of prayer for a particular intention to one member of my saint posse usually helps restore peace in my heart. At first, I considered the Our Lady, Undoer of Knots, one of my favorites, who is favored by Pope Francis and who has been a proven provider of grace in my life. However, the Holy Spirit kept nudging me to attempt a fifty-four-day Rosary novena. By nudging I mean, I was at a church I'd never been to, at an event I hadn't expected to attend, when I woman I'd never met handed me a small, blue, well-worn book, entitled, *Rosary Novenas to Our Lady*, which was devoted to the fifty-four-day Rosary novena. So, this, clearly, seemed to have been inspired.

While I love the Rosary and the novena, trying to put the two together for nearly two months seemed a little daunting. But unable to shake the inspiration, I sat down on my couch to begin the prayers for day one. Before I even finished the opening prayer, my heart felt a second nudge from the Holy Spirit to go outside. To which I replied, "Thanks, Lord, but I am not a big fan of being outside. There are bugs out there, and I don't like to walk in my neighborhood because the busy, narrow streets have no sidewalks and can be somewhat dangerous. Nope, I will just sit all comfy on this couch and pray. Thanks for asking." However, my mind could not formulate the first prayer because the pull outside was too great. "Seriously, Lord?" I thought. It was July, and the air outside was really warm.

I finally relented to the Spirit, grabbed my flip flops (obviously I was not prepared for any walking) and went outside to find myself a nice shady place to sit. The Spirit was not having any part of that plan; nope, it was clear to me that I was supposed to walk. Not fond of walking the busy roads surrounding my home, I decided I would make use of the fork-in-the-road on which I lived and walk in a very large circle around the perimeter of my yard. Think about Joshua and friends and the walls of Jericho! (Joshua 6)

Not being a person to willing disobey the Holy Spirit's movement in my heart, as I have learned from experience that doesn't always work out well for me, I started to walk. The first few days I hit the yard in my flip-flops, strolling very leisurely, but by the end of the two months, I was out taking the laps with my sneakers fully laced. The Lord used these fifty-four days to bring me many blessings, and while some of the moments of grace were too mystical to even begin to put into words, there came a plethora of insights I can share.

Oh, That's What Is Wrong with Me

First, my mysterious illness turned out to be menopause, making a slightly early appearance and with a vengeance. Every article I perused and book I read regarding menopause listed exercise as one of the best ways to help alleviate symptoms, and help it did. "Funny way to answer my prayer, Lord, but since it worked, I will take it." While this battle would be ongoing for a few more years, I can credit walking and prayer to greatly reducing my anxiety about the many (now-no-longer-mysterious) changes overtaking my body.

I even got over my dislike of the outdoors and found it easier to focus on the mysteries of the Rosary without the phone, television, or beckoning housework to distract me. God delighted me with butterflies just as I thought of them, and dandelions, which despite my husband's best efforts, kept popping up to greet me.

Dandelions, quite frankly, make me smile. I see in them great tenacity. They are everywhere and so very hard to be rid of. The yellow flowers are bright and cheery, but interestingly however, they need to stay rooted in order to remain in that state. In death, the dandelion experiences its most far-reaching accomplishment, spreading its seed far and wide. Each time I encountered a dandelion on my walk, I was reminded, that this is how I longed to be in my ministry work and in the sharing of the faith. Cheery and bright, but rooted; tenacious and unhampered by death to continue to spread the message of God's love and mercy.

God reminded me again and again that I was being a silent witness to my faith as I walked day after day with my rosary beads dangling from my hands. Some of the fruit from my walks included meeting a neighbor I had never met before and having another neighbor text me prayer requests. One elderly neighbor sweetly pointed out how "stupid" I looked going around in circles in my yard. *Thanks, Bob.* I prayed a little extra for him. I surely gave pause to more than one person as they passed by, and, hopefully, seeing me inspired them to say a prayer as well.

Sometimes It Takes a Tractor-Trailer-Sized Message

The thing is, I really thought that with all this focused prayer, our troubles of 2015 would magically resolve. However, other than the health realization, the rest of the difficult situations persisted with some additional horrendous new circumstances. As I entered 2016, my anger with God was about to come to a head. One morning, I hit the Rosary path ready to have it out with him.

It is important to be able to visualize my prayer path to get the full effect of what was about to happen. I live on a fork-in-the-road; so my normal route was up one road, across the back of my yard, turn onto another road that had me facing a busy highway, then across my driveway. I repeatedly circled my yard, as if it were a track.

This day as I made the circuit, I looked to heaven and aired my grievances. "Lord, what do you want from me? I never miss Sunday Mass; I've been diligently praying the Rosary for months now; I have even dedicated my life to telling people how awesome you are, and this is my reward? My life is a mess! The last six months have been plagued with so many hardships—deaths, financial struggles, and family stress! Again, Lord, I ask, what do you want from me?"

As I turned the corner of the backyard leg of my path to face the highway, I looked up to see a huge, tractor trailer driving past my home. On the side of the truck was the word—FIDELITY!

"Fidelity? Faithfulness? Is that what you want? I mean, it feels like that would be a note from you being it is a fancy Latin-rooted word?" How could I ignore the timing of that truck's appearance? That was a "godcidence" moment if ever there was one in my life. "Faithful, I can be that. I will continue to pray, hope, and wait on you, Lord."

It was my turn to decide, like Peter and the other apostles, if, when things are beyond my understanding, I will go too. "Wherever shall I go, Lord? Only you offer me the promise of bringing good in all these circumstances. Whatever the resolution, Jesus, I trust in you. I shall remain faithful in my prayer, and my hope shall remain in you."

What If I Don't See Anything

The hardest part was staying faithful as my prayers went unanswered and Jesus seemed to go silent. Although I did not ask for the Fidelity truck sign, the Lord clearly knew I needed it to help me not to lose hope. As this sign renewed my hopes, I could not help but remember the scene in the upper room when Jesus showed Thomas his wounds. It was only after Thomas had proof that he believed. He did not trust his own senses but needed to see with his own eyes. "Jesus said to him [Thomas], 'Have you come to believe because you have seen me? Blessed are those who have not seen and have believed'" (John 20:29).

Sadly, I, too, often doubt as Thomas did, though I strive to allow hindsight to remind me of God's faithfulness to me and how truly trustworthy he is. They are blessed who do not see and yet believe, but I am sure I'll still need an occasional butterfly or Fidelity truck to keep me on track.

An Invitation to Share

1. Consider how each of your senses is employed during the Mass. Reflect on some of your favorite Mass moments or memories. Be sure to include any thoughts on the emotions evoked during your reflection. In what ways do you feel that engaging more of your senses assists in your worship?

_____

_____

_____

_____

_____

_____

_____

_____

_____

_____

2. Have you spent any time in Eucharistic adoration? Do you go on a regular basis? What do you do when you are in adoration? What would you consider to be some benefits of spending even a brief fifteen minutes in prayer before the Blessed Sacrament?

_____

_____

_____

_____

_____

_____

_____

_____

_____

_____

3. Do you believe that the Eucharist is the real presence of Jesus? Do you think that if you had been standing with St. Peter and the other disciples when Jesus spoke of being the "bread of life," that you would have fled with the others, or remained like St. Peter, proclaiming, "Master, to whom shall we go? You have the words of eternal life" (John 6:68).

_____

_____

_____

_____

_____

_____

_____

_____

_____

Closing Prayer

Heavenly Father, for so long I have lived only part of your promise for my life. For so long I have loved only the least amount necessary to satisfy my desire for a relationship with you. Lord, you want more for me and from me. In your love for me, you want all of me. You long for full communion with me, but my fears and my doubts have kept me from accepting this great gift.

My heart overflows with gratitude for the gift of the Eucharist in which you invite me into a deeper communion with you. You are offering me a gift so wonderful, that if angels could be jealous, St. Maximilian Kolbe tells us, reception of the Eucharist would be the object of that jealousy.[21] Yet, I do not always embrace this wondrous grace as I should. My human senses struggle to recognize that you are always around me throughout nature, alive in the Scriptures, and present most especially in the bread and wine consecrated during the celebration of the Mass.

You promise that if I seek with my heart, you will be found; if I ask, you will answer; and if I knock, the door will be opened. Lord, I seek, I knock, and I beg. May I be yoked to your teachings and accept your blessings beyond measure. As I enter into this final week of study, may I be willing to discover all the more the invitations you have given me that have brought me to this place of faith. As I read the next chapter, may I be inspired to consider where you are calling me to share these great gifts. Lord, may your grace be sufficient in my quest to be closer to you and to be an instrument to others in discovering your great love.

Dear Lord, be with me in my reading and reflection as I grow ever closer to you. Amen.

7: Invitation to Go Make Disciples

INVITATION

Opening Prayer

Jesus, my gift to you for all you have given me, is to share your love with others. The abundant gifts of grace, hope, faith, and mercy, to name just a few, have transformed my life. How could I possibly keep them to myself and still honor your generosity?

The gift of friends to share my spiritual journey has blessed me beyond measure. The opportunity to share my thoughts and inspirations, as well as being able to learn from their great wisdom, has produced much fruit in my spiritual life. I am so grateful that you have not called us to take this journey of faith alone. I pray that I will always be open to accepting invitations to come and know you better. Lord, give me the courage to reach out to the women you place in my life to invite them to know you better as well.

It is clear to me, Lord, that you do not give the gift of faith to keep for ourselves, but to go forth and share. When I am feeling it a strain to be hospitable, send your grace to open wide my heart to welcome as you would welcome. Inspire within me new ways to share the Good News. Give me the words to speak, the compassion to share always with love, and the insight to know where

*you wish it to be shared. Send forth your Spirit; let it move with me, so
I may be a worthy and dependable instrument in your hands. Amen.*

On My Heart

_____

_____

_____

_____

_____

_____

_____

_____

_____

_____

_____

Invitation to Go Make Disciples

A faithful friend is a sturdy shelter (Ben Sira 6:14) as is a faith-filled
friend. A friend who is willing to take this journey of faith with you,
someone willing to encourage you in your practice of the faith—that
is a real treasure. The one who lifts you up when you are spiritually
dragging and reminds you to pray when you don't feel like it. Imagine,

then, the treasure one finds in friends who not only possess all the aforementioned amazing attributes but who also share the desire and are even eager to discover more about Jesus through prayer, sacrament, and Scripture.

I am blessed with an amazing sturdy shelter in my life, and it comes in the form of my weekly faith-sharing group. The women in this group are some of my dearest friends, who meet every Monday and share their struggles, their sorrows, and their triumphs as they journey closer to Jesus. Our faith-sharing group has been such a gift. There are nights filled with laughter, and there are other nights when we shed tears together. We use technology to stay connected during the week and, most especially, for sharing prayer requests.

This group has helped me develop better prayer practices—just knowing that they are counting on me the next week always helps me push through my procrastination or busyness to make sure I find time to complete my reading. However, life does happen, and I do not always find that time to complete my planned reading. Another benefit of meeting with a group is that even when I have not been able to prepare, I can count on someone else to have covered the material. While on my own I may just give up on completing the book once I fall behind, with the group I can get caught up in one night, and pick up with the next chapter. I always think that even without having read the selections, it is better to attend the meeting so I can allow the Lord to touch my heart through the others rather than to avoid the meeting, and take away the opportunity to learn something that Jesus wants to teach me that week.

Faith-sharing groups are a powerful experience of faith, one that I know has transformed my own spirituality and is the reason I feel so passionate about helping other women connect with or create their own small (or large) groups. Blessed for years with this shared faith experience, I would say the three greatest benefits of joining together with others on your spiritual endeavors are:

- ☙ *accountability for remaining committed to growing in relationship with Christ;*

- ☙ *learning from the wisdom, experiences, and faith of others on the same journey; and*

- ☙ *encouragement and enjoyment that this shared adventure offers each of us.*

The irony is I nearly missed out on growing in faith with these incredible women because I hate cleaning. To host the group at my home each week, I felt that I had to have the house in company-clean condition. There is a vast difference between being company clean and family clean. There is an added responsibility in preparing the home for company that includes being more thorough than simply dust bunny wrangling. Honestly, it can be exhausting, especially when you lack the hospitality gene, which some women who host and serve other so naturally just seem to come by. In 2013, after hosting a few studies, I had decided that although I enjoyed the fellowship and accountability for studying God's Word, it was time to abdicate my facilitator throne.

My plan was to finish out the summer, to wait until at least I had returned from World Youth Day in Rio de Janeiro in July, before announcing my plans. As I have shared, that pilgrimage was quite the experience, filled with so many blessings and transformative encounters with Christ. Our group concluded our pilgrimage with a Mass celebrated by Cardinal Sean O'Malley of the Archdiocese of Boston. The Gospel that day included the story of Martha of Bethany opening her home to Jesus (Luke 10:38). Cardinal O'Malley ended his homily with these powerful words, which I am fairly sure were meant for me, "If you want to truly change the world, if you want to be faithful evangelizers, then you must open your hearts and your homes, and learn hospitality" (Cardinal O'Malley's quote paraphrased from my memory and notes from the homily).

Upon returning home, instead of announcing that I could no longer host the faith-sharing group, I made a different announcement. From that day forward the group would enjoy coffee, tea, and water on me, and they could count on finding my home in family-clean condition. My focus would be on sharing the Word of God with them and enjoying our spiritual reading and conversation without my Monday anxiety about cleaning. I promised that no one would be skeeved out by the bathroom nor would they be attacked by a dust bunny army, but they may find dishes in my sink and laundry in the hallway. What a relief it was to hear that no one expected me to be the biblical Martha, or Martha Stewart; they were just grateful for my willingness to continue opening my home. I am so grateful for the Holy Spirit's spiritual 2×4 during the World Youth Day closing Mass. I sometimes wonder which of the many blessings would have been missed if I had given into my weariness of hosting that summer and had canceled our group. More often, however, I am grateful to God that I heeded the message received during that closing Mass and continued to receive his bountiful grace.

Invitation to Ponder

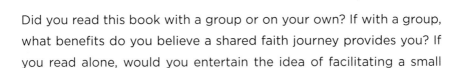

Did you read this book with a group or on your own? If with a group, what benefits do you believe a shared faith journey provides you? If you read alone, would you entertain the idea of facilitating a small group at your parish or in your home? How does, or can, the Lord use others to deepen your relationship with him?

_____

_____

_____

_____

_____

_____

_____

_____

_____

_____

_____

_____

Connecting to Scripture

PRAYER TO THE HOLY SPIRIT BEFORE READING SCRIPTURE

Come, Holy Spirit. Fill me with every grace and blessing necessary to understand the message, prepared for and awaiting me, in the Scriptures. May I grow deeper in faith, in hope, and in love with Jesus as I spend this time with the Word of God. Amen.

⑦ Sirach (Ben Sira) 6:14-17 _____

_____

_____

⑦ Matthew 28:16-20 _____

_____

_____

⑦ Luke 10:38-42 _____

_____

_____

⑦ John 4:35-42 _____

_____

_____

⑦ John 12:1-8 _____

_____

_____

⑦ Hebrews 13:2 _____

_____

_____

I'm always moved by the last paragraph of Matthew's gospel—the version in my Revised Standard Version, Didache Bible, titles this paragraph, "Jesus Commissions the Disciples" (Matthew 28:16–20). In this concluding passage, Matthew shares how the eleven disciples went to Galilee as Jesus had told them, and when they saw him, they worshipped him, but some doubted. This alleviates some of the guilt of my own doubts. If they're looking at him and doubting, how much harder is it for us? But yet the Apostles teach us, among many other things, that through the grace of God bestowed through the Holy Spirit, we can overcome these doubts. Even more important, in the midst of their doubts, they went forth and made disciples of nations as Jesus had instructed them. We, too, despite our doubts, or lack of trust in our abilities to share the faith, can go forth empowered by grace to help others know the truth of Christ.

Conversion from Sinner to Saint

One of my favorite Scripture stories is about the woman at the well; the Eastern Rite Church calls her St. Photini. Giving her a name makes it easier for me to feel a personal connection to her, and it also makes it easier to add her to my saint posse. What draws me to her story is the relationship she has with Jesus and how that encounter with him converts her and opens her heart to share what he has done for her with others. He first meets her at the well in the middle of the day. That would not be a typical time for a woman to go to the well to draw water. It would be hot, and the well would be very empty. She was clearly looking to be by herself at that well. It's in this lesson that we learn that Jesus meets us right where we are. And then he doesn't start to berate her for her sins and her failings, but he engages with her in conversation and shows her what he has to offer her—the living water. Once he has begun building this relationship by presenting what he has to give, then he calls for her to take a closer look at her life and start to see how she can better that life. He invites us to come and see and to follow him by showing us all that he has to offer. When we look through the Scriptures, we see that they are filled with his promises and his abundant blessings for us.

I suppose Scripture also includes these directives to change our behaviors because they're not good for us. How hard it is for us to understand that Jesus wants what's best for us. St. Photini embodies that. We see the progression of her relationship with Christ from rabbi to prophet to Messiah. It's a slow progression of Jesus inviting, befriending, and instructing, all with great love. Teaching her, and us, how to become more closely united with the Father, and then to be transformed by our encounters with Christ. With every encounter you have with Jesus, you are never truly the same again. Even what you may believe to be the most insignificant meeting with Christ—perhaps in a time of prayer, participation in a sacrament, or reading the Scriptures—never leaves you the same person than before you entered into those grace-filled activities. Every single moment with Jesus is a moment of conversion.

St. Photini, once filled with that knowledge, understanding, and wisdom that Jesus bestowed on her, could not keep it to herself. She went out and told others. The beauty of evangelization is summarized in this verse from John's Gospel: "Many more began to believe in him because of his word, and they said to the woman, 'We no longer believe because of your word; for we have heard for ourselves, and we know that this is truly the savior of the world'" (4:41–42). That is what we are called to do in our invitation to go out and share the good news; merely invite others to know Christ by sharing the authentic witness of what Jesus has done for us.

While we can follow Jesus' model of sharing the Good News by meeting people right where they are, as he did with the Samaritan woman at the well. Sometimes we may be asked to go a step further and to be willing to open not just our hearts but our homes. We may be called out of our comfort zones to extend hospitality and provide faith-sharing opportunities for others to be able to come and know the abundant graces Jesus has waiting for us all. What great joy when our friends and relatives and kinsfolk return to us after their own encounters with Jesus saying, "We believe he truly is the Savior of the world, not because you told us but because we have seen and heard the truth for ourselves."

The Better Part

There was more that Mary and Martha would teach me besides the blessing of hospitality, and that was the importance of making time to slow down and listen to Jesus. "[Allison, Allison,] you are anxious about and troubled about many things. There is need of only one thing. Mary has chosen the better part and it will not be taken from her" (Luke 10:41–42).

Okay, so Jesus didn't actually say, "Allison, Allison," but sometimes I know that as I read the Scriptures, Jesus is speaking right to my heart. While I am certainly not Martha, I am worried about a great many things. The better part in my life, aside from sitting at Jesus' feet during my time in Eucharistic adoration, is making the time every Monday night to gather together with my friends and collectively sit with Jesus and learn from him.

That is the good portion. That is the blessing the Jesus wants all of us to have, to spend time at his feet. And because I'm involved in a study, it's not just Mondays that I give to Jesus, but to prepare for our time together, I read on, at least, one or two other nights each week. Additionally, my prayer life improves because my time in study makes me all the more mindful of Jesus. I find myself conversing with him daily, even multiple times a day, moving ever closer to St. Paul's goal of praying without ceasing (1 Thessalonians 5:17). The choicest perfume I have to offer Jesus is my time, and like Mary of Bethany, I desire to anoint Jesus with the finest thing I have to offer.

Your Turn

The invitations have been extended. The encounters with Jesus through the "grace trifecta" have begun. The conversion of hearts and transformation of our faith have been set in motion. Now what? What will you do with the blessings God in his grace has bestowed upon you during this time together in his Word? Will you accept the invitations to:

- *come and see;*

- *take his yoke;*

- *know the gifts of God;*

- *ask in his name;*

- *forgive from your heart;*

- *believe in him; and, most especially,*

- *go and make disciples in his holy name?*

An Invitation to Share

1. Think about the women you typically encounter in your life—they could be family, friends, neighbors, coworkers, or acquaintances at church. List three whom you would like to invite to participate in your next book or Bible study faith-sharing group. What obstacles do you need to overcome to extend these invitations? Pray to Our Lady, Undoer of Knots to help remove those obstacles.

_____

_____

_____

_____

_____

_____

_____

_____

_____

2. Is there someone in your saint posse who inspires you to take what Jesus has taught you and share it with others? What is it about this saint's life that is most inspirational to you? If you have yet to discover your heavenly role model, consider an internet search for a new saint friend. List activities, interests, or keywords that would be most helpful in your search.

_____

_____

_____

_____

_____

_____

_____

_____

_____

3. Which invitation in *The Gift of Invitation* surprised you? Which invitation did you feel most closely connected to? Which invitation would you like to explore further in order to take Jesus up on living it better in your life?

_____

_____

_____

_____

_____

_____

_____

_____

_____

Closing Prayer

Refreshed by my time with you, Lord, may I put into practice all you have shown me in these pages. May the many lessons you have blessed me with enrich my life, my private prayer, and my sharing of the faith with others. May I embrace the wondrous gift of adoption into your holy family through my Baptism, by writing the date of my Baptism on my calendar and in my heart and celebrating daily what an amazing gift that day is in my life.

May I often come to you in prayer, striving to learn how to pray without ceasing, allowing my work, chores, silence, and even my leisure to be a prayer to you. May I always be in constant communion with you. May our relationship flourish as I spend more time with the Scriptures and in receiving the outward signs of your grace in the sacraments. May the Word of God live richly within me, always on my mind, in my heart, and on my lips.

May your perfect love wipe away my fears and anxieties. Please increase your grace within me so I may continue to seek, ask, knock, and accept all your invitations with a heart full of hope. During these last seven weeks, you have presented me with a new way to grow and trust in you. Jesus, I believe that by standing on the Word of God, I am able to ward off the spiritual attacks that keep me from fully trusting in you and living in the peace you came to leave with me.

May I never forget that your grace is always sufficient in whatever needs I have, that your love and mercy are my refuge when the storms of life rage against me. Lord, inspire my heart to go and make disciples, and to share all you have done for me and in my life. May the witness of my faith glorify you and encourage others come to know, love, and serve you, my Lord and my God.

Dear Lord, please continue to be with me in my lifelong journey to accept your glorious invitations as I grow ever closer to you. Amen. Alleluia.

Endnotes

1 Saint Augustine, *Saint Augustine's Confessions* (Lafayette, IN: Sovereign Grace Publishers, Inc., 2001), Book 1, p. 1.

2 Recommendations can be found on my website, www.Reconciled-ToYou.com.

3 For more information on the other titles available in the *Stay Connected* series visit www.gracewatch.media.

4 *The Gift of Invitation* is the first book in the *Stay Connected Journals for Catholic Women* series from Gracewatch Media.

5 From the Revised Standard Version of the Bible, via "Tecarta Bible" App.

6 Though this story is quoted across the internet in many amusing variations, the actual source remains a mystery. Regardless of whether spunky St. Teresa said it or not, the heart of this story not only fits her persona but also expresses how many of us have surely felt on our own journeys with God.

7 St. Catherine Laboure encountered three apparitions of the Blessed Virgin Mary in 1830. On November 27, the lady showed St. Catherine the miraculous medal. She commissioned St. Catherine to have one made and to spread devotion to this medal. St. Catherine died on December 31, 1876, and was canonized on July 27, 1947. Her feast day is November 28.

8 Joseph F. Schmidt, *Everything Is Grace: The Life and Way of St. Thérèse Lisieux* (Ijamsville: Word Among Us Press, 2007).

9 Maria Faustina Kowalska, *St. Faustina's Diary,* 1320. www.thedivine-mercy.org.

10 "Have no anxiety at all, but in everything, by prayer and petition, with thanksgiving, make your requests known to God. Then the peace of God that surpasses all understanding will guard your hearts and minds in Christ Jesus" (Philippians 4:6–7).

[11] *Star Trek,* 1996.

[12] Rich Mullins, "Awesome God," 1988.

[13] Phil Vischer and Lisa Reed, *God Is Bigger Than the Boogie Man* (A VeggieTales Book), (Nashville: Candy Cane Press, 1995).

[14] John Paul II, "Closing of World Youth Day Homily of the Holy Father John Paul II, Tor Vergata, Sunday 20 August 2000," Vatican website, July 18, 2018, http://w2.vatican.va/content/john-paul-ii/en/homilies/2000/documents/hf_jp-ii_hom_20000820_gmg.html.

[15] For more, including step-by-step instructions, visit www.ignatianspirituality.com.

[16] R. Scott Hurd, Forgiveness: *A Catholic Approach* (Boston: Pauline Books and Media, 2011), p. 6.

[17] Earworm courtesy of Disney's *Frozen,* 2013.

[18] Hurd, *Forgiveness,* summary of chapter 2. Quotes from Kindle edition, locations 225, 1373, and 247 of 1559.

[19] Hurd, *Forgiveness,* p. 8.

[20] Thomas Aquinas, "Prayers and Devotions: Tantum Ergo." USCCB.org. http://www.usccb.org/prayer-and-worship/prayers-and-devotions/prayers/tantum-ergo.cfm (accessed May, 20, 2018).

[21] Msgr. Charles Pope, "If Angels Could be Jealous...."(June 3, 2010), adw.org. http://blog.adw.org/2010/06/if-angels-could-be-jealous (accessed July 18, 2018).